PERFECTIONISM
AND GIFTED
CHILDREN

ROSEMARY CALLARD-SZULGIT

ILLUSTRATED BY

MARK K. SZULGIT

SCARECROWEDUCATION

Lanham, Maryland, Toronto, and Oxford

2003

Published in the United States of America
by ScarecrowEducation
An imprint of The Rowman & Littlefield Publishing Group, Inc.
4501 Forbes Boulevard, Suite 200, Lanham, Maryland 20706
www.scarecroweducation.com

PO Box 317
Oxford
OX2 9RU, UK

British Library Cataloguing in Publication Information Available

Library of Congress Cataloging-in-Publication Data

Callard-Szulgit, Rosemary, 1946–
     Perfectionism and gifted children / Rosemary Callard-Szulgit.
        p. cm.
     Includes bibliographical references and index.
     ISBN 1-57886-061-X (pbk. : alk. paper)
     1. Gifted children—Education—United States—Psychological aspects.
     2. Gifted children—United States—Psychology. 3. Perfectionism
     (Personality trait). I. Title.

     LC3993.2 .C36 2003
     371.95—dc21   2003009792

The paper used in this publication meets the minimum requirements of
American National Standard for Information Sciences—Permanence of
Paper for Printed Library Materials, ANSI/NISO Z39.48-1992.
Manufactured in the United States of America.

To Greg, who was never really forgotten in the first book and is loved and adored as much as all our family members.

To Karl, my husband, who has always encouraged and supported me in all my endeavors with Eric, Fern, Greg, and Mark, our wonderful family.

To Mom, Josephine Eastman Stiles Callard, and Dad, Chesbro W. Callard. They were wonderful parents and gave us their very best.

Thank you, Brenda.

CONTENTS

PREFACE

I am a recovering perfectionist. I never realized I was until twenty-five years ago, when I began teaching a self-contained fourth-grade class of gifted children in a suburban school district in Rochester, New York. Within two days, I was stunned to see personality traits of my students identical to those of myself. I saw so much of myself in my students—not wanting to make a mistake, not realizing when enough was really enough (in projects and creative activities), concentrating on the perfect grade rather than enjoying the learning, fearful of using my sense of humor (in case my thoughts would not really be funny), never feeling I was smart enough (in third grade I tested post–high school in all the achievement test scores), giving too much credit to what others thought rather than what I was thinking or creating, worrying about things that in reality were not that important (age and hindsight are wonderful teachers). On and on the list proceeds.

I also saw all the wonderful traits I admire and appreciate in gifted nine-year-olds—wide-eyed innocence; loving, caring kindness; energy; a strong sense of morality; musical talents; artistic, sensitive, intuitive talents; highly reflective thinking abilities; shyness; gregariousness; leadership; wanting to be accepted; wanting to be cared for; wanting to please; avoiding work that required thinking (they were used to getting A's because they already knew the material). On and on this list goes too—positive qualities and inspirations of all children!

Perfectionism is a wound. It hurts immensely and casts a cloud even on the sunniest of days. It can affect self-worth, relationships in families, relationships at work, even playing and having fun.

My intention is not to present a gloom-and-doom picture about perfectionism. A sunny day with clouds here in Arizona is still a beautiful day. Enjoying a round of golf at Club West with my husband is still exhilarating. My intention is to help gifted children and their parents gain a better understanding of perfectionism and how it affects their lives. It is sometimes hard to begin healing when we are not aware that a wound exists.

Besides, I can honestly now say, I am a recovering perfectionist. Clouds, errors, and less-than-perfect jobs accomplished do not stress me (or at least only minimally compared to twenty-five years ago)! I worked hard to reach this stage in my life. How I accomplished this and other suggestions are contained in chapter 6, How to Recover from Perfectionism.

I have also included a chapter entitled Who Are the Gifted and Talented? There continues to be a misunderstanding about gifted children and how to serve them educationally. We now know that what works for gifted children works for all children. We know that using an inclusive process rather than an exclusive program is a much healthier way to assimilate the education for our gifted children in schools, avoiding the labels of "gifted" and "not gifted," "you're in, you're out." We are erasing the dividing lines between the supposed "haves" and "have-nots." Teachers cannot do it alone. Parents, administrators, and volunteers must help. As the school days demand increased responsibilities, our educators are desperately trying to serve children with a multitude of thinking levels and emotional development in their classrooms.

All children deserve to be educated at their cognitive levels. All children deserve to be happy and joyful. All children deserve to thrive in their accomplishments and creative endeavors. No child should hurt, and perfectionism hurts!

May this book provide all of you reading it with the understanding and support you need to love and nurture your wonderful children, working positively with your schools and educators, and undoing any negative effects of perfectionism. You can do it. I did.

I will help you every step of the way.

1

WHAT IS PERFECTIONISM?

Throughout my career in education, I have vehemently and continually
stated that the number-one social and emotional issue gifted children
need to deal with is perfectionism. Perfectionism hurts. It not only hurts
physically and emotionally, but it can interfere with relationships with family, peers, teachers, coaches, siblings, neighbors, roommates, colleagues,
business partners, friends, and self.

I am a recovering perfectionist. I can laugh when I say it now, but I spent
many of my younger years suffering with the pain of perfectionism. I can
clearly remember the Sunday I was playing "Toccata and Fugue in F Minor."
I was twelve years old and the organist at the First Presbyterian Church in
Medina, New York. I made a chord mistake and spent the afternoon crying
on my bed because I was such a failure in my own mind and heart. Every
week, between the ages of twelve and eighteen, I prepared the organ music
for the Sunday services. Can you imagine? I thought I was a failure because
I would make an occasional playing error. Now I wonder how I could even
assume that much responsibility at such a young and vulnerable age.

Generally, perfectionists are people who are very bright and who have
succeeded because of their high intelligence and talents. They often can see

many solutions to one problem. They can create and not feel comfortable with a finishing point, always knowing more could be done. Many times, perfectionists will avoid new experiences, due to a fear of failure. They're afraid others will view them as inadequate.

Perfectionists have exceedingly high expectations—for themselves and for others. On a personal level, this can lead to a workaholic syndrome. On a social level, personality conflicts can ensue at work and at home. Gifted children often have the talents to assume adult roles. They are often multipotential. These precious youngsters need guidance with making choices and managing their time.

Children can learn perfectionism from their parents and their interactions with them. Such children measure parental acceptance by their perfect deeds and avoid areas where mistakes might be made and a loss of love might occur.

With proper counseling, perfectionists can be helped to lead a more balanced and realistic lifestyle. I'm not sure there is a complete cure for perfectionism, but recovery is possible.

I am a recovering perfectionist.
—Rosemary S. Callard-Szulgit

What is perfectionism? Where does it come from? Can it be genetic, or is it solely environmentally influenced? How does this condition affect those people labeled perfectionists? Is it truly deleterious? Doesn't our society encourage everyone to be the best they can be? What can be done for perfectionists? Why do those not afflicted with perfectionism sometimes wish to be more perfectionist?

Misunderstandings in our society regarding perfectionists are prevalent. The life of a perfectionist is fraught with fears, misgivings, and the never-ending feeling that things are not quite good enough. Perfectionists must deal with problems ranging from paralysis to workaholism. In a perfectionist's mind, more is never enough, and his best is never the best.

Imagine that your identity and self-concept are attached simply to the products you produce—school assignments, your work performance, or your personal appearance. Imagine that after work each day, as you drive home, you review only the mistakes you made. They may have been only small mistakes that affected no one, like the way your plans for the day were written or something you said to a coworker. To the perfectionist, errors are what the day was all about. Imagine that the only time you have a good day is when you make no mistakes. Since this is almost impossible, you can understand that a perfectionist rarely has a good day.

Hess (1994, 29) defines perfectionism as the pursuit of excellence taken to the extreme. Perfectionists often impose a great deal of pressure on themselves. They believe that they should be able to do the impossible. Some people may attempt to attain flawless results in only one area of their lives, whereas others may try to attain perfection in several areas that are important to them. These unrealistic and unreasonable goals only perpetuate perfectionists' problems by setting them up for the thing they fear most: failure—and fail they must, because the goal they are striving for is impossible to achieve (Hess 1994, 28–29).

Burns, cited in Adderholdt-Elliott (1990), states that perfectionists are those whose standards are high beyond reach or reason, people who strain compulsively toward impossible goals and who measure their own worth entirely in terms of productivity and accomplishment. For these people, the drive to excel can only be self-defeating. Perfectionists partake in their own version of fortune-telling. They immediately assume the worst will happen. The affects of this are sometimes self-fulfilling.

Some research points to environmental and societal factors as the precursors to the development of perfectionists. Children are not only affected by the expectations that parents have for them but also by the expectations parents have for themselves. If children grow up watching parents demand perfection of themselves, they may model that behavior. Burns, cited by Hess (1994, 29), states that children whose parents are perfectionists feel a loss of love and acceptance from their parents when they make mistakes; they learn to avoid mistakes in order to gain parental love and acceptance. As a result, the children become perfectionists too, avoiding mistakes even when they are no longer seeking anyone's approval but their own.

Our society surrounds us with cues that perfection is a desired state. In the media, in movies, and on billboards, the ideas of perfection in beauty, career, and family are constantly touted. Perfectionists internalize these messages to a greater degree than others because their own expectations are so high (Hess 1994, 29). While challenged to be perfect, they are stymied by the fact that this can never be achieved. For the perfectionist, this realization translates not into a message of reality, as it does for nonperfectionists, but instead into a message that they are a social failure.

Nurture or nature? Is perfectionism contagious? Inherited? Environmental? Initial physical and mental capabilities are inherited. Perfectionism can be self-induced or learned from the environment. It can manifest in many forms by a misguided parent, guardian, mentor, or peers. The unfulfilled ambitions of one or all these individuals can reinforce a gifted child to emulate someone else's faded dreams. A desire to please authority figures, loved ones, or peers geometrically progresses with each success and each positively reinforced adulation. In this scenario, the perfectionist child is not entirely responsible. He has become the victim of another's fancy.

Roeper, cited by Adderholdt-Elliott (1990, 50), states that perfectionism has been found especially in gifted children and adults, because the gifted are better able to approximate perfectionism and thus it is rewarded in them. Hess (1994, 28) tells us that perfectionists are often very bright people who are accustomed to success and are afraid of failure, perhaps because of their lack of experience with it.

Gifted and talented young people are so often intent on meeting their goals that they refuse to acknowledge their limitations, often pushing themselves to succeed even when they may be out of their league (Bernardo 1990, 30).

Teenagers, especially those in competitive, upper-echelon schools and who are very bright, compare themselves with peers who may be even more intelligent and then start to feel there is something wrong with them, that they can't make the grade.

Because of their desire to attain perfection, these people often encounter many roadblocks throughout their lives. Most of these problems lead to underachievement. This is interesting, as perfectionists are often thought of as overachievers. A common problem of perfectionists is procrastination.

Adult perfectionists may also become workaholics. Because their internal locus of control is not secure, their self-esteem is tied to external rewards (Adderholdt and Goldberg 1999, 21). Adolescent perfectionists often experience great anxiety when it comes time to choose a career path. They are so fearful of not choosing the right career or failing at the one they do choose that they may choose one that is not intellectually challenging or emotionally rewarding for them. The Karnes and Oehler-Stinnett study indicates that gifted youth experience greater stress than nongifted youth in the areas of achievement, social status, and career aspirations. Many gifted youth delay making career choices because they fear making a less than perfect choice (Emmett and Minor, 1993, 351).

Emmett and Minor (1993, 357–58) found that perfectionists were most concerned with (a) the best preparation for the future and the most potential for future advancement; (b) not being ordinary (the desire, need, or both, to accomplish more in one's career than the average person); (c) ability (in most cases, the concern that one does not have great enough ability for a particular occupation); (d) making a difference (work must be meaningful and make a difference in the lives of human beings); (e) sense of accomplishment; and (f) true to self. It is of utmost importance that parents, teachers, and counselors recognize that this is untrue. Gifted and talented children must be afforded the same availability of services as their nonidentified peers. When their emotional needs are being met, the children will be able to more realistically define their goals.

When perfectionism is taken to an extreme, the result can be suicide. Weisse (1990, 353) cites research by Webb, Meckstroth, and Toan indicating that gifted children do seem more likely to show signs of depression, particularly if they have not been identified as gifted or have not received support for their feelings. Current school programs that meet the needs of the gifted student decrease this type of problem.

Perfectionism is not a terminal condition. Parents and educators can be helpful in addressing the problems of young people suffering with perfectionism. Acknowledging and addressing their own pursuit of perfection can help, if that is one of the precipitators of the problem.

I agree wholeheartedly with Gardner (1993): "The less a person understands his own feelings, the more he will fall prey to them. The less a person understands the feelings, the responses, and behaviors of others, the more likely he will interact inappropriately with them and therefore fail to secure his proper place within the larger community." Helping children recover who are severe perfectionists is quite a challenge. As an educator and parent, what a wonderful privilege!

Keep reading; I'll show you the ways.

MEDLEY ON GIFTEDNESS

The following songs are by Kelly Jordan.

(To the tune of "The Lion Sleeps Tonight")
In the classroom, the mighty classroom, the gifted sleep today,
In the classroom, the mighty classroom, the gifted sleep today.
Oh why can't we see their needs?
Oh why, if we're not supported?
They need our help, they need our help, they need us more than ever.
Now our gifted students are special students, that need some special
education.
Oh, our gifted students are special students, that need some special
education.
Oh how are we going to do it?
Oh how, if we're not supported?
They need our help, they need our help, they need us more than ever.

(To the tune of "The Brady Bunch")
Here's the story, of our gifted students, and how they really are so
    misunderstood.
Like that one about the global giftedness, that really is quite rare.
And then there's IQ, does it depend on it? Not necessary for the art and
    music gifted.
Yes, I said art and music are a gifted domain; they're not just some little
    talent.
Then there's always debate, how is one gifted?
Some say genes while the others say environment.
I say both contribute to our students, they have a gift that needs to be
    developed.
They need encouragement, from some adults, for they're not as well
    adjusted as they seem.
They need encouragement, they need support.
For those gifted ones are truly not simply "talented."

"The Perfectionist's Rock-n-Roll"
(To the tune of "We Will Rock You")
You've got too much to do, not enough time.
Don't even want to start 'cause it'll never be right, 'cause
You are, you are, a perfectionist, a perfectionist.
Yes, you are, you are, a perfectionist, a perfectionist.
You put work before play, every day,
Give no thought to losing a night of sleep 'cause
You are, you are a perfectionist, a perfectionist.
Yes, you are, you are, a perfectionist, a perfectionist.
One day you win, and you're feeling high.
The next day you can't believe you didn't get an A, 'cause
You are, you are, a perfectionist, a perfectionist.
Yes, you are, you are, a perfectionist, a perfectionist.
You miss the happy moments, always looking back,
Or thinking what should you do in the days ahead, 'cause
You are, you are, a perfectionist, a perfectionist.
Yes, you are, you are, a perfectionist, a perfectionist.

(To the tune of "Twinkle, Twinkle, Little Star")
Now our semester is almost done, and Rosemary wants to know what
    we've learned.
We know those myths and what's a perfectionist,
But in my opinion, there's got to be more.
Let's go back to our schools and spread the word,
Our gifted students are special, and they need special services.

2

WHO ARE THE GIFTED AND TALENTED?

By definition, the U.S. Department of Education reflects today's knowledge and thinking about gifted children (Ross 1993, 26):

> Children and youth with outstanding talent perform or show the potential for performing at remarkably high levels of accomplishment when compared with others of their age, experience, or environment.
>
> These children and youth exhibit high-performance capability in intellectual, creative, and/or artistic areas, possess an unusual leadership capacity, or excel in specific academic fields. They require services or activities not ordinarily provided by the school.
>
> Outstanding talents are present in children and youth from all cultural groups, across all economic strata, and in all areas of human endeavor.

Whether you choose to support the use of this definition or not, the fact remains that there are hundreds and thousands of children in our schools and homes whose thinking and comprehension abilities far surpass the norm of their peers.

Critics of gifted education services often posture that all children have gifts.

I agree completely! I believe we all have our own special gifts. I personally love my red hair. I love my stepdaughter's exceeding generosity, intelligence, beauty, and work ethic. I love my neighbor's willingness to talk and walk daily with me. I love our second daughter's beauty, kindness, and honesty. Indeed, we all have many gifts. Thousands of children in our schools, however, also far surpass their classmates in cognitive (thinking) abilities. As teachers, we have the responsibility of educating all children at their appropriate cognitive levels. To do less would be unconscionable. This can be done through differentiation, compacting, independent study, and acceleration, combined with enrichment.

In the past, the problem with exclusive programs was you were either gifted or not. An inclusive process for educating the gifted is so much better and healthier than an exclusive program in our educational system. We can service all kids, including the gifted, without isolating anyone.

All children need to be loved, protected, and nourished emotionally and intellectually. All children need to play and laugh. They need to express themselves and have their thinking and talents supported. Gifted children are no different. Their needs are the same as those of all other children—and more.

Throughout my career, I have encountered more misperceptions and myths about gifted children than I care to remember, hear again, nor have nightmares over. I just couldn't believe what my ears were hearing. Many educators and parents would discuss their perceptions about the gifted, such as: They're conceited. They're unsociable. They're introverted. They're less healthy than their peers. They're physically weaker. They have poor eyesight. They don't fit in. They have problems developing. And so on.

I would continually be shocked, miffed, angry, and downright irritated when hearing these ridiculous comments, especially because the people saying them actually believed and repeated them as educational truths!

Educating the Gifted: An inclusive process rather than an exclusive program.

Winner (1996) does a fine job of describing the nine most prevalent myths surrounding gifted children and very aptly provides the realities associated with them, as follows:

Myth 1: Global Giftedness. The underlying assumption here is that gifted children have a general intellectual power that allows them to be gifted across the board. Scholastic giftedness is often not a global capacity that cuts across the two major areas of scholastic performance: language (oral and written) and mathematics. Children can even be gifted in one academic area and learning-disabled in another.

Myth 2: Talented but Not Gifted. While children who are precocious in the kinds of skills assessed by an IQ test are called gifted, children who show exceptional ability in an art form are called talented. There is no justification for such a distinction. Artistically or athletically gifted children are not so different from academically gifted children.

Myth 3: Exceptional IQ. IQ tests measure a narrow range of human abilities, primarily facility with language and numbers. There is little evidence that giftedness in nonacademic areas, such as art or music, requires an exceptional IQ.

Myths 4 and 5: Biology versus Environment. Where does giftedness come from? The commonsense myth is that giftedness is entirely inborn. Diametrically opposed to this view is the myth, held by some psychologists, that giftedness is simply a matter of intensive training by parents and teachers begun at an early age. This view ignores the powerful role of biology in determining whether there is any gift for the environment to develop.

Myth 6: The Driving Parent. Some people assert that gifted children are "made" by overzealous parents intent on their children's stardom. It is true that parents of gifted children are often highly involved in the nurturance of their children's gifts. But such an unusual degree of investment and involvement is not a destructive force. It is a necessary one if a child's gift is to develop.

Myth 7: Psychological Health. Gifted children often face ridicule, taunts of being nerds or geeks. Most children easily pick out the awkward, unathletic loners, or the show-offs with strange interests out of touch with those of their peers. Psychologists have countered this view with an idealized picture of high-IQ children as popular, well-adjusted, exceptionally moral, and glowing with psychological and physical health.

But children's prejudices may strike close to the truth. We seem to have a need either to deny or to idealize the gifted. Gifted children are often socially isolated and unhappy, unless they are fortunate enough to find others like themselves. The vision of the well-adjusted gifted child applies only to the moderately gifted child and leaves out the extremes.

Myth 8: All Children Are Gifted. Many principals and teachers assert that all children are gifted. Sociological consideration of the concept of giftedness has sometimes led to the conclusion that giftedness is just a social construction to buttress elitism. No one seems to mind the fact that children gifted in music routinely take advanced classes outside of school. But the view that all students are gifted in school skills leads to adamant positions against any form of special education for the gifted. In reaction, parents of the gifted turn to support groups and talk of how misplaced egalitarianism discriminates against their children and makes them stressed as well as bored. When special education for the gifted is offered, it is minimal and is fashioned to fit the moderately gifted. Gifted children have special needs no less than do retarded or learning-disabled children. Moreover, they are our human capital and promise of our future.

Myth 9: Gifted Children Become Eminent Adults. Gifted children are typically seen not only as creative children but also as future creative and eminent adults. But many gifted children, especially prodigies, burn out, while others move on to other areas of interest. Some, while extremely successful, never do anything genuinely creative. Only a very few of the gifted become eminent adult creators. The factors that predict the course of a life are multiple and interacting. Over and above level of ability, important roles are played by personality, motivation, the family environment, opportunity, and chance.[1]

Ellen Winner reaches out to a large audience, managing to debunk the myths surrounding gifted children in a coherent and intellectually stimulating way. She starts by identifying the atypical characteristics of gifted children: precocity, a rage to master (a particular domain), and a tendency to march to the beat of their own drum. These characteristics, along with the general definition of gifted children cited earlier, set these children apart from their peers. *Gifted Children: Myths and Realities* is a wake-up call for teachers, parents, and administrators—all who deal in the education of children. I began using this text in my graduate course "Teaching the Gifted K–12," and my students continue to extol its worthiness. *Gifted Children:* It belongs on all school and home bookshelves—along with my two books, of course!

---

[1]Excerpted from *Gifted Children: Myths and Realities* by Ellen Winner. Copyright © 1996 by Ellen Winner. Reprinted by permission of Basic Books, a member of Perseus Books, L.L.C.

Acceleration
and/or
Enrichment
and/or
Compacting
and/or
Differentiation
=
Meeting Gifted Students' Instructional Needs

Many gifted children want to do, see, and hear everything in sight. They have the ability to think and comprehend well beyond their years, and they want to experience it all, and all at once. I used to silently chuckle to myself when many of the students in my self-contained gifted classes would get teacher and parent approval for their long-term research and creativity projects, only to want to switch midstream to pursue other creative ideas!

Parents and teachers can play a huge role in helping gifted children set realistic goals, stay focused, and manage their time wisely. These skills become even more critical as children approach middle and high school years. I deal with time management and study skills extensively in chapter 4 of my book, *Parenting and Teaching the Gifted*. You'll find some good tips there.

I still vividly remember the evening five years ago, when one of my graduate students presented Stephanie Tolan's "Is It a Cheetah?" for his article review. I ran up to the front of the class when he finished and kissed his cheek! Ms. Tolan couldn't be more right than she is with her cheetah metaphor! I hope every teacher, administrator, and parent in the world reads this essay soon. I reprint it here.

IS IT A CHEETAH?

It's a tough time to raise, teach, or be a highly gifted child. As the term *gifted* and the unusual intellectual capacity to which that term refers become more and more politically incorrect, the educational establishment changes terminology and focus.

Giftedness, a global, integrative mental capacity, may be dismissed, replaced by fragmented "talents," which seem less threatening and theoretically easier for schools to deal with. Instead of an internal developmental reality that affects every aspect of a child's life, "intellectual talent" is more and more perceived as synonymous with (and limited to) academic achievement.

The child who does well in school, gets good grades, wins awards, and "performs" beyond the norms for his or her age is considered talented. The child who does not, no matter what his innate intellectual capacities or developmental level, is less and less likely to be identified, less and less likely to be served.

A cheetah metaphor can help us see the problem with achievement-oriented thinking. The cheetah is the fastest animal on earth. When we think of cheetahs, we are likely to think first of their speed. It's flashy. It's impressive. It's unique. And it makes identification incredibly easy. Since cheetahs are the only animals that can run 70 mph, if you clock an animal running 70 mph, it's a cheetah!

But cheetahs are not always running. In fact, they are able to maintain top speed only for a limited time, after which they need a considerable period of rest.

It's not difficult to identify a cheetah when it isn't running, provided we know its other characteristics. It is gold with black spots, like a leopard, but it also has unique black "tear marks" beneath its eyes. Its head is small, its body lean, its legs unusually long—all bodily characteristics critical to a runner. And the cheetah is the only member of the cat family that has nonretractable claws. Other cats retract their claws to keep them sharp, like carving knives kept in a sheath—the cheetah's claws are designed not for cutting but for traction. This is an animal biologically designed to run.

Its chief food is the antelope, itself a prodigious runner. The antelope is not large or heavy, so the cheetah does not need strength and bulk to overpower it. Only speed. On the open plains of its natural habitat, the cheetah is capable of catching an antelope simply by running it down.

While body design in nature is utilitarian, it also creates a powerful internal drive. The cheetah needs to run!

Despite design and need, however, certain conditions are necessary if it is to attain its famous 70-mph top speed. It must be fully grown. It must be healthy, fit, and rested. It must have plenty of room to run. Besides that, it is best motivated to run all out when it is hungry and there are antelope to chase.

If a cheetah is confined to a ten-by-twelve-foot cage, though it may pace or fling itself against the bars in restless frustration, it won't run 70 mph.

Is it still a cheetah?

If a cheetah has only 20-mph rabbits to chase for food, it won't run 70 mph while hunting. If it did, it would flash past its prey and go hungry! Though it might well run on its own for exercise, recreation, fulfillment of its internal drive, when given only rabbits to eat, the hunting cheetah will run only fast enough to catch a rabbit.

Is it still a cheetah?

If a cheetah is fed zoo chow, it may not run at all.

Is it still a cheetah?

If a cheetah is sick or if its legs have been broken, it won't even walk.

Is it still a cheetah?

And finally, if the cheetah is only six weeks old, it can't yet run 70 mph.

Is it, then, only a "potential" cheetah?

A school system that defines giftedness (or talent) as behavior, achievement, and performance is as compromised in its ability to recognize its highly gifted students and to give them what they need as a zoo would be to recognize and provide for its cheetahs if it looked only for speed. When a cheetah does run 70 mph, it isn't a particularly "achieving" cheetah. Though it is doing what no other cat can do, it is behaving normally for a cheetah.

To lions, tigers, leopards—to any of the other big cats—the cheetah's biological attributes would seem to be deformities. Far from the "best cat," the cheetah would seem to be barely a cat at all. It is not heavy enough to bring down a wildebeest; its nonretractable claws cannot be kept sharp enough to tear the wildebeest's thick hide. Given the cheetah's tendency to activity, cats who spend most of their time sleeping in the sun might well label the cheetah hyperactive.

Like cheetahs, highly gifted children can be easy to identify. If a child teaches herself Greek at age five, reads at the eighth-grade level at age six, or does algebra in second grade, we can safely assume that child is a highly gifted child. Though the world may see these activities as "achievements," she is not an "achieving" child so much as a child who is operating normally according to her own biological design, her innate mental capacity. Such a child has clearly been given room to "run" and something to run for. She is healthy and fit and has not had her capacities crippled. It doesn't take great knowledge about the characteristics of highly gifted children to recognize this child.

However, schools are to extraordinarily intelligent children what zoos are to cheetahs. Many schools provide a ten-by-twelve-foot cage, giving the unusual mind no room to get up to speed. Many highly gifted children sit in the classroom the way big cats sit in their cages, dull-eyed and silent. Some, unable to resist the urge from inside even though they can't exercise it, pace the bars, snarl and lash out at their keepers, or throw themselves against the bars until they do themselves damage.

Even open and enlightened schools are likely to create an environment that, like the cheetah enclosures in enlightened zoos, allow some moderate running but no room for the growing cheetah to develop the necessary muscles and stamina to become a 70-mph runner. Children in cages or enclosures, no matter how bright, are unlikely to appear highly gifted; kept from exercising their minds for too long, these children may never be able to reach the level of mental functioning they were designed for.

A zoo, however much room it provides for its cheetahs, does not feed them antelope, challenging them either to run full out or go hungry. Schools similarly provide too little challenge for the development of extraordinary minds. Even a gifted program may provide only the intellectual equivalent of 20-mph rabbits (while sometimes labeling children suspected of extreme intelligence "underachievers" for *not* putting on top speed to catch those rabbits!). Without special programming, schools provide the academic equivalent of zoo chow, food that requires no effort whatsoever. Some children refuse to take in such uninteresting, dead nourishment at all.

To develop not just the physical ability but also the strategy to catch antelope in the wild, a cheetah must have antelopes to chase, room to chase them, and a cheetah role model to show them how to do it. Without instruction and practice they are unlikely to be able to learn essential survival skills.

A recent nature documentary about cheetahs in lion country showed a curious fact of life in the wild. Lions kill cheetah cubs. They don't eat them, they just kill them. In fact, they appear to work rather hard to find them in order to kill them (though cheetahs can't possibly threaten the continued survival of lions). Is this maliciousness? Recreation? No one knows. We only know that lions do it. Cheetah mothers must hide their dens and go to great efforts to protect their cubs, coming and going from the den under deep cover or only in the dead of night or when lions are far away. Highly gifted children and their families often feel like cheetahs in lion country.

In some schools, brilliant children are asked to do what they were never designed to do (like cheetahs asked to tear open a wildebeest hide with their claws—after all, the lions can do it!), while the attributes that are a natural aspect of unusual mental capacity—intensity, passion, high energy, independence, moral reasoning, curiosity, humor, unusual interests, and insistence on truth and accuracy—are considered problems that need fixing.

Brilliant children may feel surrounded by lions who make fun of or shun them for their differences, who may even break their legs or drug them to keep them moving more slowly, in time with the lions' pace. Is it any wonder they would try to escape, would put on a lion suit to keep from being noticed, would fight back?

This metaphor, like any metaphor, eventually breaks down. Highly gifted children don't have body markings and nonretractable claws by which to be identified when not performing. Furthermore, the cheetah's ability to run 70 mph is a single trait readily measured. Highly gifted children are very different from each other, so there is no single ability to look for, even when they are performing; besides that, a child's greatest gifts could be outside the academic world's definition of achievement and so go unrecognized altogether. While this truth can save some children from being wantonly killed by marauding lions, it also keeps them from being recognized for what they are—children with deep and powerful innate differences as all-encompassing as the differences between cheetahs and other big cats.

That they may not be instantly recognizable does not mean that there is no means of identifying them. It means that more time and effort are required to do it. Educators can learn the attributes of unusual intelligence and observe closely enough to see those attributes in individual children. They can recognize not only that highly gifted children can do many things other children cannot, but that there are tasks other children can do that the highly gifted cannot.

Every organism has an internal drive to fulfill its biological design. The same is true for unusually bright children. From time to time the bars need be removed, the enclosures broadened. Zoo chow, easy and cheap as it is, must give way, at least some of the time, to lively, challenging mental prey.

More than this, schools need to believe that it is important to make the effort, that these children not only have the needs of all other children to be protected and properly cared for, but that they have as much right as others to have their needs met.

Biodiversity is a fundamental principle of life on our planet. It allows life to adapt to change. In our culture, highly gifted children, like cheetahs, are endangered. Like cheetahs, they are here for a reason; they fill a particular niche in the design of life. Zoos, whatever their limitations, may be critical to the continued survival of cheetahs; many are doing their best to offer their captives what they will need eventually to survive in the wild. Schools can do the same for their highly gifted children.

Unless we make a commitment to saving these children, we will continue to lose them and whatever unique benefit their existence might provide for the human species of which they are an essential part.

—Stephanie S. Tolan

Author's note: Please disseminate this widely if you find it useful. Proper attribution would be appreciated, however.

From "Is It a Cheetah?" Copyright © Stephanie B. Tolan. Used with permission. Ms. Tolan's Website is www.stephanietolan.com.

THE AUTONOMOUS LEARNER MODEL

In his Autonomous Learner Model, Betts (1986) presents an excellent overview of the behaviors, feelings, and needs of gifted children in the following six profile types:

Type One, The Successful. These gifted children learn well, know the system, display the appropriate behaviors, score high on achievement and intelligence tests, are identified as gifted, and are eager for approval and acceptance. These types often become bored with school, have not learned how to pursue their own interests, and are dependent on teachers and other adults for direction. Type Ones are often underachievers throughout life.

Type Two, Divergently Gifted. Gifted children in this group are usually quite creative, do not conform to the system, question authority, and seldom receive recognition, honors, or rewards. Type Twos struggle with self-esteem and are frustrated by lack of affirmation from their schools. They may also be at risk for drug addiction, bad behavior, or dropping out.

Type Three, The Underground. This group of children go underground to hide their giftedness—girls in middle school and boys in high school—deferring to athletics. Pressure from significant adults only tends to increase Type Threes' resistance.

Type Four, The Dropouts. Type Fours are angry with the system and adults in their lives who have not met their needs. School is irrelevant to them. These gifted children generally have low self-esteem and benefit from a close, trusted adult. Traditional schooling generally does not work for Type Fours, and family counseling as well as individual counseling are critical for their eventual happiness and success.

Type Five, The Double-Labeled. This group of gifted children are physically or emotionally handicapped or both. Their learning behaviors are not consistent with the traditional behaviors schools look for in gifted children. Type Fives' weaknesses are often the focus of traditional school systems.

Type Six, The Autonomous Learner. Once gifted children become autonomous learners, they are independent, self-directed, goal-oriented risk takers. Type Sixes do not depend on others to chart their course in life; they do it for themselves.

Many times common sense eludes gifted children. Teachers and parents can easily become exasperated with them, wondering why such intelligent kids can be so lacking in common sense.

Being gifted has nothing to do with common sense. Giftedness has to do with the ability of children to perform or show the potential for performing at remarkably high levels of accomplishment when compared with others of their age, experience, or environment (Ross 1993, 26). Common sense is more likely linked to gifted children's learning styles. Lacking common sense would more likely be linked to having an abstract learning style.

TeaCHer TWiSTeR

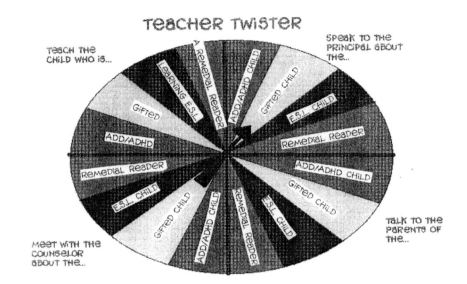

Teach the
child who is...

Speak to the
principal about
the...

Talk to the
parents of
the...

Meet with the
counselor
about the...

- Comes complete with interchangeable tiles to fit your classroom needs!

 Now, new and improved to include gifted students!

- Are you tired of feeling pulled in too many directions at once? Then Teacher Twister is for you! With just one spin of the spinner, you'll know exactly what to do!

ASPERGER'S SYNDROME AND
TWICE-EXCEPTIONAL CHILDREN

Coupled with myths surrounding gifted children, there also seems to be growing confusion among gifted children, those with Asperger's Syndrome, and twice-exceptional children.

Asperger's Syndrome is defined by Goldberg-Edelson (1995) as follows:

> For [the Asperger's Syndrome] diagnosis to be made, there must be quali-
> tative impairment in social interaction, as manifested by at least two of the
> following: marked impairment in the use of multiple nonverbal behaviors
> (e.g., eye contact, gestures); failure to develop age-appropriate peer rela-
> tionships; lack of spontaneous seeking to share interest or achievements
> with others; lack of spontaneous achievements with others; lack of social or
> emotional reciprocity; restricted, repetitive, and stereotyped patterns of
> behaviors, interests, and activities, as manifested by at least one of the fol-
> lowing: preoccupation with at least one stereotyped and restricted pattern
> of interest to an abnormal degree; inflexible adherence to nonfunctional
> routines or rituals; stereotyped and repetitive motor mannerisms; and pre-
> occupation with parts of objects. There must additionally be clinically
> significant impairment in social, occupational, or other functioning; and
> clinically significant delay in language cognitive development, adaptive be-
> havior, or in curiosity about the environment. (2)

Little (2002, 59) helps clear up some of the common misunderstandings and confusion between gifted traits and Asperger's Syndrome traits in the following table:

Asperger's Advanced Vocabulary:	Gifted:	Twice-Exceptional:
Unaware of another's perspective	Advanced vocabulary	Advanced vocabulary
Literal thought	Ability to see another's viewpoint	Unaware of another's perspective
Poor language comprehension	High abstract thinking skills	Intensity of focus
Intensity of focus	Good language comprehension	Sensory sensitivity
Introverted	Intensity of focus	Introverted
Excellent memory	Introverted	Enjoys "rote" exercises
Sensory sensitivity	Excellent memory	Poor language comprehension
	Sensitivity toward others	

The author does note that there are many commonalities among the lists, and the reader should note what motivation is behind each behavior.

I feel it is critical to clear up some of the misunderstandings coupling gifted and Asperger's, so that gifted children are not simply lumped into a special education label, which seems to be currently happening with many educators.

One of my friends has a wonderfully gifted four-year-old son who is currently being treated for Asperger's. What I find appalling is that Chris was told by his son's psychologist that 80 percent of gifted children have Asperger's. I was so enraged when I heard that statistic quoted that I asked for the documentation and research to validate that statement. Neither I nor Chris have received copies of such research, and I have encouraged Julia to find a different psychologist!

If you review Little's list, you'll note a distinction between a child with an advanced vocabulary who is unaware of another's perspective and a child with an advanced vocabulary and the ability to see another's viewpoint. Literal thought is certainly different from high abstract thinking skills.

It has been my experience throughout my career in gifted education that the majority of gifted kids are far more extroverted than introverted, so I need to challenge that item on Little's list.

For the general characteristics of gifted children based on my experiences, please note the following:

Common Characteristics of Gifted and Talented

- Able to express self easily, succinctly and without hesitation. Many times we need to help them "cushion" their responses in respect for others' feelings
- Accomplished across a broad range of skills
- Easy recall of facts and mastery of knowledge presented
- Has a delightful sense of humor, understands and appreciates wit
- Intense concentration and attention in area(s) where interested; can become highly focused and absorbed
- Keen sense of what's right, and often sees issues as either black or white
- Likes to assume leadership roles
- Loves learning
- Nonconformist
- Perfectionist
- Persistent (some refer to as stubborn)
- Possess specific academic aptitudes
- Procrastinator
- Questioning, curious, inquisitive
- Reads several years above grade-level expectations
- Sensitive, intuitive
- Sets high goals and standards for self
- Takes pleasure in inductive learning and synthesis (creativity)
- Verbal (very)

I hope this chapter has helped you gain a better understanding of who our gifted and talented children are. We need to dispel the myths surrounding gifted education and gifted children and accept and educate all children with their educational needs.

I'll finish reading this chapter right after school, Mrs. Smith…I mean right after soccer practice, and my music lesson, and dinner, and after I play my new Harry Potter video game with my little brother, and after my friend Susan calls me, right after my bath…

3

COMMON NEGATIVE
BEHAVIORS OF
PERFECTIONISTS

I don't believe I've ever underestimated the abilities and creativity of gifted children, but they have never ceased to amaze me! This has also been true of my graduate students throughout the years. One of the five major assignments in EDI 651, Teaching the Gifted K–12, is a creativity project worth 30 percent of the total grade. The graduate students are completely flummoxed the first night of class, when we review the semester's work. They have no idea what they'll do as a creative activity to share with their classmates. I promise them they'll not only have one idea, but two or three, after our first four or five classes, when they've begun assimilating all the information discussed, shared, read, and presented. I tell them to absolutely not worry until then. If they still don't have an idea by the fifth class, I promise them, I'll suggest they begin worrying!

The latter has never happened, and the last three weeks of classes, when creativity projects are presented, have always been the most popular classes of the semester. The same is true throughout our educational endeavors. Once we take all children to the synthesis level, the true excitement of learning and creating kicks in, and the personal ownership supports pride in every child.

There are many ways that gifted children can be creative but not always in positive ways. When it relates to perfectionism and the avoidance of work assignments, relationships, and self-worth, gifted children's creative capacities for thinking can be a hindrance.

Throughout my thirty-five-year career, I have noticed the following seven behaviors gifted children seem to use as protection mechanisms. They are pretty creative!

I'M JUST NEVER GOOD ENOUGH

For years, I suffered from feeling that I was just not smart enough—there was so-o-o-o much more to learn. Even with all the awards I earned academically and musically throughout my schooling, I always felt that I could have done better! During my graduate studies, I finally became tired of completing research papers three or four times longer than anyone else's. What hurt was that those students all received A's as well! I deliberately drew the line and handed in a research paper that had minimal information rather than what I "knew" would make it perfect.

Wouldn't you just know? I received an A+. The professor recognized my paper as exemplary in the class. From that day forward it was a bit easier to feel that what I did was good enough. Phew—what a relief!

THE TRIPLE Q: QUANTITY OR QUALITY = QUANDARY

Severe perfectionists just don't know when to stop. Because of their abilities to think and create well beyond the norm, these children have a very hard time drawing an assignment or project to a close. The "system" also helps perpetuate a need for quantity. I never understood why college professors put a minimum page requirement on research papers or other thinking assignments. If we're looking for quality and creativity, then numbers shouldn't count. I love it when I can award an A++ to one of my graduate students with a succinct, creative, and brilliant presentation! Hurrah!

FUN? WHAT'S THAT?

I grew up never really knowing how to have fun, for two reasons. First, I was in all the advanced academic classes, was first chair clarinet in band and orchestra, and was in marching band (we performed at all the football games, rather than relaxing and having fun at them). I accompanied our A-6 high school choir and was church organist at the First Presbyterian Church, performing every Sunday from ages twelve through eighteen. Fun? I don't think so. I certainly didn't learn how to have fun during my growing-up years.

Second, as a perfectionist, even if I did have brief moments of fun with games or events, I was worrying if I'd make a mistake or people would think I just wasn't good enough. You'll be happy to know that, as a recovering perfectionist, I now can have oodles of fun on the golf course, enjoy long, solitary walks, and enjoy presenting at major conferences and consulting on this very topic of perfectionism.

I can now truly say, "Life is fun!" If any of you golfers don't believe me, just invite me to the Masters Tournament with you next year, and I guarantee I'll have the best time of my life!

GOLD, BRONZE, SILVER, AND HONORABLE MENTION AWARDS

The perfectionist wants all the honors—gold, bronze, silver, and honorable mention. He needs all the awards to be perfect. If he is awarded a gold medal with a winning composite score of 9.87 and the silver award goes to a competitor with a score of 9.80, then the perfectionist has failed in his mind. He could have beaten his fellow competitor by .20 points, rather than just .07. Also, he wasn't perfect, was he? After all, 10.0 is the perfect score!

Such destructive behavior continually pulls your self-esteem down, and it certainly doesn't help with social and peer relationships.

NOW AND WHEN SYNDROME

This behavior is so self destructive. Your initial goal is the carrot. You obtain it, but the carrot is not the very best one in the batch; two carrots are better than one; and certainly five carrots are even better! You forget your original goal. You chastise yourself for errors or flaws in accomplishments. You beat this irrational horse and yourself as a perfectionist to death.

You reached a successful conclusion. You have your carrot. You did it. If you missed one hurdle during the race, you still came through and succeeded. Enjoy your moments of glory.

RANDOMLY ROLLING A BALL

If you continuously and randomly roll a ball, it doesn't move forward unless it is directed by a focused force. Thomas Alva Edison performed his experiment over and over again until he "saw the light" and reached his "perfection" or successful conclusion. From each failure he learned and pursued a different tactic until he succeeded. Even Ivory soap isn't 100 percent pure!

VACILLATING GOLF GAMES, SO TO SPEAK

You golf your very best game ever; you're thrilled; you're exhilarated; you tell all your friends; you're filled with pride. Next time out, you miss your record score by eight. You're bummed; you're a terrible golfer; how can you be so bad? All the glory of your previous record is thrown into a sand trap, and you bury your successful feelings from the day before. So high one day, so low the next.

You can't eagle every hole. Life hands you bogeys, pars, and birdies. That simply is life, so work on enjoying the fun and camaraderie of the game.

Mandy Durr

Workaholic Kid

Amidst, the pandemonium of the first jazz rehearsal, the lead tenor sax player (gifted/perfectionist) wants to make sure he is in tune.

4

THE POSITIVES
OF PERFECTIONISM

None
Nil
Nada
Zip
Ninguno
Kein
Aucun
Nikt
Clum
Ingen
Babu
It translates the same in any language.

Kelly Jordan '02

5

THE NEGATIVES
OF PERFECTIONISM

Both Delisle (2002) and Adderholdt and Goldberg (1999) distinguish between persons with unhealthy perfectionist tendencies striving for an impossible ideal and persons who strive to achieve and succeed without becoming dysfunctional. They refer to the latter process as the "pursuit of excellence."

The example occurring most often in my self-contained classroom of gifted children that distinguished between perfectionism and the pursuit of excellence was the occurrence of a B+ grade rather than an A. Some children would be absolutely devastated with a B+, yet a B+ meant very good. Very good just wasn't good enough. Only the "perfection" of an A was acceptable to them.

I must admit I was the same way growing up. Even receiving an A- was torturous to me. I really did consider myself a failure.

Following are several patterns of perfectionism I saw regularly with many of my gifted students:

- Avoidance of trying anything new for fear of failure.
- Receiving straight A's on the report card and not being satisfied because you're not first in the class.

- Not playing team sports unless in a key position, such as pitcher or center.
- Being angry with others who make mistakes. How could they be so stupid? Why aren't they perfect?
- Having to keep everything at home in perfect order. Clutter, even one paper amiss, is unacceptable. Can you imagine having a mother who wouldn't allow one speck of dirt in the kitchen or one dirty dish in the sink? Problems lie ahead for her children—and for her!
- Spending hours practicing an instrument or training for a sport for two primary reasons: trying to be the best and avoiding being with other people so you won't be "caught" making a mistake.
- Reading only the assigned books to help ensure an A, not wasting time reading additional or self-enjoyed materials.

Contrast these perfectionism patterns reworked into patterns in the pursuit of excellence:

- Take a chance, try something new, have fun, possibly make a mistake, and know that it really isn't a bad thing; you're normal, just like the rest of us!
- If grades really do reflect "what you don't know," learn the information you're supposed to, and move on without feeling like a failure for being less than perfect.
- If you like a team sport, join, do your best, practice, learn cooperation, learn team skills, get more physically fit, and benefit from dozens more learnings you'll get from being involved with a team.
- Do these people become so angry with you? Cool it! They don't expect you to be perfect, so give them and yourself a break!

One of my nephews just couldn't believe all my paper piles and random clutter. I couldn't believe he and his mother's severe need for cleanliness and order. Somewhere among the three of us was a happier balance, for them and those living with us.

For some gifted children, there is a fine line between practicing excessively to become accomplished, perfect, and better than anyone else, compared to performing with excellence, being proud of who you are, succeeding, and enjoying yourself while doing so.

So many of our children have lost their joy for reading, often due to excessive amounts of time being spent on homework and misuse of time. I talk more thoroughly about the misuse of homework and positive solutions to this problem in my book *Parenting and Teaching the Gifted*.

Another reason students are not reading for pleasure is their focus on achieving top grades and not reading anything other than the assigned materials. Imagine helping our perfectionists and all students rekindle their love for reading! We could all go to sleep at night with extra sweet dreams!

Some common behaviors and characteristics of perfectionists are the following:

- Procrastinate
- Isolate themselves from family and friends so that "mistakes" can't be perceived
- Hide their sense of humor, in case someone might not really think it's funny
- Are highly critical of others
- Are highly critical of self
- Are very controlling
- Can't have fun or really enjoy a game because they must try to win
- Are extremely sensitive
- Don't know where to draw the line in completing assignments (there's always more to think, know, and do)
- Find it hard to be team players
- Focus on the one thing that is wrong rather than the multitude of things that are right
- Are chronic worriers
- Take a "sick day" on the day a major assignment or project is due
- Feel that enough is never enough
- Take on more tasks than they can ever realistically do or do well in the allotted amount of time
- Have poor time management skills
- Need reassurance constantly
- Have low self-esteem, feel never quite good enough
- Are always giving gifts and trying to please
- Are judgmental, see things as black or white
- Are insecure
- Call themselves stupid when they make even the smallest mistake
- Have a very orderly routine

The most disconcerting aspect of perfectionism for me before "recovery" was living in a continual state of anxiety. If a teacher, friend, or parent made a suggestion to me or pointed out an error, I would simply be crushed. I couldn't just listen, be thankful for the added expertise, adjust, monitor, accept, and move on. My very soul hurt. Granted, I put myself on the extreme end of the perfectionist scale, but there are tens of thousands of gifted children paining right now, just like I did.

Often there is a discrepancy between gifted children's intellectual abilities and their emotional rationalities.

Just as I did, many gifted kids don't allow themselves mistakes because brightness to them means not being allowed to make a mistake.

I've always been highly intuitive. I would know what was going on in other people's lives before they did. The mistake I made was trying to tell them. Now I've learned to basically keep my mouth shut, unless people ask, although my brothers and husband might disagree.

Coupled with strong intuition often comes extra sensitivity. Correcting gifted children can often be the same as inflicting a painful wound. They have striven so hard to be and make everything perfect that "helpful" words are perceived as painful rejections. The children interpret your message as everything's wrong and may not even hear all your compliments. The focus is on what is wrong.

It's not hard to understand that a gifted child's emotional maturity may not match his intellectual achievement, nor even that of his peers—so much is going on in his head!

I continue to stress that we can help and help we must. Talking, walking, counseling, and caring—these all work!

Hi, Uncle Bob!

Mom I need help with my science homework!

Science Homework
Calculate how many psi of Helium we will need for our hot air balloon ride down Letchworth gorge next week.

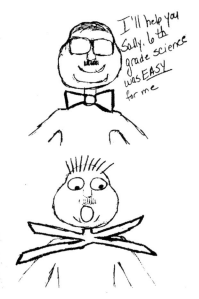

I'll help you Sally. 6th grade science was EASY for me

6

HOW TO RECOVER FROM PERFECTIONISM

I am a recovering perfectionist. Recovery is possible. Honest. Following are a few examples of arduous, time-consuming behaviors I remember which eventually helped me pursue recovery.

During my freshman year at SUNY Potsdam, I would write weekly letters to my friend at Notre Dame University. The letters would be five or six pages long. If I erred, sometimes I would rewrite the entire page(s), just so the letter would be perfect! The letters did look nice, but what a ridiculous waste of time. Of course, with e-mail now, corrections are so much easier. ☺

In eighth grade advanced English class, we were assigned a major poetry project. I had always been a procrastinator, but I did get my work in on time. On one particular assignment, I just couldn't stop. There was so much poetry to report on, and I didn't know where to draw the line. The day my assignment was due, I stayed home "sick" and finished my project—104 pages! I did earn an A+. Most of my classmates received A's, and the second longest report in class was ten pages. Somehow, I think my peers were having much more fun with their "extra" time than I was at home, writing and writing and writing.

I always remember not thinking or knowing I was pretty when I was young. I was a 5-foot-10-inch redhead, 133 pounds, with beautiful clothes and a pretty good figure. I was so consumed with trying to be perfect in every aspect of my life that I never really enjoyed the compliments I received or the attention given my way. When I first began teaching, one of my good friends and colleagues took me to a local mall, sat me down, and said, "Start watching all the people going by. Tell me when you see someone with hair as pretty as yours, a complexion as nice, anyone as tall and slender as you, or anyone you see who's prettier." Sitting there with Jo was a reality eye-opener for me. From that time on, I gave myself a glimmer of credit for being somewhat attractive. ☺

These examples are reasons why gifted children and perfectionists need counseling time—to help develop or keep or modify their reality base. Because of their incredible abilities to think and create, gifted children can develop numerous scenarios around one thought and continue to expand on the theme.

I've also learned how to laugh! I was always so serious and focused, I never really thought too much was funny. Now I can even laugh at myself for being that ridiculously serious in my younger years. Once I decided I wanted to lighten up on myself, I would practice randomly smiling. Then, when I was at a meeting and a majority of people laughed (even if I didn't think what was said was funny), I figured it was a good cue to at least "practice" laughing and smiling. Practice does make perfect and, since I was recovering, I was only going for better. ☺

To my credit, I was always a risk taker and never seemed to settle for the routine or the norm. Many of my family members and friends wondered why I wanted to pursue change and wasn't satisfied with the status quo. While their opinions slowed me down a bit, I was usually able to continue forging ahead on my own. A good example is when I decided to buy my first home in the number-one school district in my area. My dad thought I was nuts to take on homeowner responsibilities as a single woman. I lived in a gorgeous apartment on East Avenue in Rochester already. I wanted to buy a home in the Brighton Central School District, so if I married and had children, they would be educated in the Brighton Schools. As a single woman, I would also feel safe. I married a man with four teenagers, and my home was robbed during my home ownership! But I doubled my money when I sold my first home just ten years later, and Dad and my younger brother did lend me the $10,000 I needed for the initial down payment. All's well that ends well!

If you're a risk taker, even though you're a perfectionist, listen to what respected others have to say, use what information or suggestions might add to your success, then press on. Don't slow down too much. You have a good sense if your ideas can succeed. If one or two don't, that's part of the reality of life. Keep going and smile on the way.

I can't emphasize enough the benefit of exercise—as a stress reducer, health builder, endorphin supplier, body detoxifier, and body toner. As one of the sole survivors and supporters of gifted education in the first school district I taught in, daily attacks were common occurrences from the community, as well as from other educators. Once I joined the YMCA and began working out rigorously, I was in a much better frame of mind each day to fend off the attacks and was better able to control my perfectionist tendencies, as well!

Worrying tends to consume a large part of a perfectionist's time and energy. Once I realized I was a chronic worrier, I would mentally ring a buzzer when I started worrying about anything, big or small. It reminded me to stop. This method did slow down my worrying. Over a year's period, I improved significantly. Writing a book that can help hundreds or thousands of children and their parents is far more gratifying than worrying about whether or not you said or did the right thing two days ago at work!

No matter what methods you try for perfectionism recovery, please do begin. You know yourself best. Use your creativity to develop your own recovery methods if mine don't work for you. Spending a day on a beautiful golf course is much nicer than staying at home trying to be perfect.

Enjoy, and happy recovery!

7

COMMONLY ASKED QUESTIONS ABOUT PERFECTIONISM

Q. Are firstborn children in families more likely to be perfectionists than other siblings?

A. Yes. Focused adult attention is a natural for firstborns. These children almost always spend more time around adults than do the successive children. As brothers and sisters come along, parents just don't have 100 percent of their time to dote on, teach, train, and model, as they did when there was just one child.

I'm sure all parents can remember checking the crib constantly and throughout the night, making sure the firstborns were breathing. By the time number two came along, we knew from experience that he or she would breathe throughout the night, with or without us checking repeatedly.

Q. Is perfectionism—about mood, weight, spending on clothes, achievement, relationships—always a negative trait? Can it be beneficial?

A. Most things in life can be beneficial, if kept in balance. It's when we approach the extremes that problems occur. Perfectionists need help understanding when enough is enough. This is where we as teachers and parents can step in and help our perfectionist students. Once we identify which of our children are perfectionists and what behaviors are associated with this, we can help set limits for them. Setting limits is a critical step in the recovery of a perfectionist. Talking and counseling can be an immense help, too!

Q. Can you explain to me just who perfectionists are?

A. Generally, perfectionists are people who are very bright and have succeeded because of their high intelligence or talents. They often can see many solutions to one problem. They can create and not feel comfortable with a finishing point, always knowing that more could be done. Many times, perfectionists will avoid new experiences, due to a fear of failure. They're afraid others will view them as inadequate.

Perfectionists have exceedingly high expectations—for themselves and others. On a personal level, these can lead to a workaholic syndrome. On a social level, personality conflicts can ensue at work and at home.

Children can learn perfectionism from their parents and their interactions with them. Such children measure parental acceptance by their perfect deeds and avoid areas where mistakes might be made and a loss of love might occur.

With proper counseling, perfectionists can be helped to lead a more balanced and realistic lifestyle. I'm not sure there is a complete cure for perfectionism, but recovery is possible.

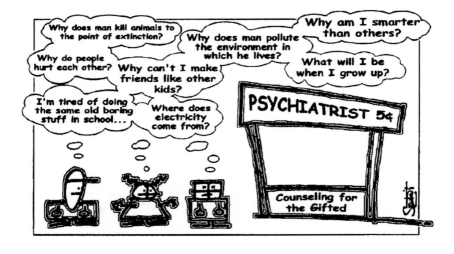

Q. Most parents would probably want this problem, but I'm not sure it's healthy. Our eleven-year-old gifted son is a straight-A student, top in his class academically, involved on the soccer team, and first chair violin in the orchestra. The problem is, Jonathan is so conscientious, he studies and practices all the time, to the exclusion of joining us on family outings, picnics, sports, games, or any other form of entertainment. We're very proud of his accomplishments, but somehow I just don't think this behavior is normal or healthy. Is it?

A. This behavior is normal for a severe perfectionist and can lead to serious emotional and physical consequences if allowed to continue over a long period of time. You're quite right that this behavior is not healthy. You need to intervene to help Jonathan with the following steps:

1. Use the time management sheets at the end of chapter four in my book *Parenting and Teaching the Gifted*. Plan times throughout the week and month that your son *will* join in with you on planned family events. The choice of outing can be his, allowing freedom and flexibility. This can certainly include watching some favorite TV shows or movies together or quiet reading time.

2. Plan regular times to sit and talk with Jonathan. Gifted children have a multitude of ideas and thoughts going on in their heads, and they benefit greatly by talking, helping keep a stable and normal balance.

3. Either utilize the services of your school's counselor or a private one of your choice for Jonathan to speak with. Many times a child is more likely to speak with a trusted professional than with a family member or favorite teacher.

4. Walk together. Walking is a wonderful stress reducer; it helps build up natural endorphins in the brain and is super as jibber-jabber time. Once you get your son beyond the initial resistance to the idea, he'll actually look forward to the time together.

5. Always let your son know you care about him. Phrases of endearment and daily hugs and touches provide an immediate and important strength and balance to the day.

Try any or all of these suggestions. I would be very surprised if you didn't notice improvement after just one or two weeks. If not, e-mail me for additional activities at szulgit2@aol.com. I'll be glad to help.

Q. Year after year after year, teachers and counselors have told my husband and me that our son is an underachiever, yet none of the teachers have been able to get him to "achieve" at their "expected levels" for him. He maintains a B average, plays sports, and seems pretty content to us. Should we be expecting more of him? We want our son to be happy, healthy, and psychologically adjusted. Are we letting him waste his potential?

A. It sounds to me like you're doing just fine in your parenting role. Many perfectionists and gifted children are emotionally devastated if they earn a grade of B, yet, by definition, a B represents an achievement that is good!

I do have to wonder if your son is achieving B's because he already knows the material and can breeze right through the assignments and tests. I am also concerned that he might be an underachiever because he is not being educated at his aptitude level, like so many of our gifted children in American schools. If this is the case, I encourage you to meet with your son's teachers and review his achievement and nationally normed scores. If his test scores indicate that he has been achieving one, two, or even more years ahead of his peers and grade-level expectations, then I suspect this is why the teachers have been suggesting underachievement to you.

Be careful with the solutions suggested. Many times, gifted children are given more work as a challenge, and this becomes the typical "punishment" for being bright! Enrichment is also overused, to the point that the overload of enrichment activities at grade levels can be seen coming out of the students' ears!

At the elementary level, compacting is an easy solution to testing children through materials they already know and getting them educated at an instructional level compatible to their achievement and aptitude. This is the positive. The negative is, often high-achieving students are given packets to work on at a higher grade level but without proper instructions and monitoring. They are often left to sit in the hall to do their assignments. This is a lonely road to walk for these students and not educationally instructive or emotionally supportive.

In middle and high schools, accelerated courses or advanced-placement courses often serve to educate the gifted and more cognitively advanced students. The positive is that high-achieving students are together and hopefully working at compatible aptitude levels. The negatives could be excessive amounts of homework and, in some districts, advanced-placement courses are not weighted, so an A in advanced calculus is weighted the same as an A in regular calculus. Cumulative averages remain the same, yet the amount and degree of work vary significantly. Class standings could be affected, as well as scholarship awards.

These are ideas to consider when you meet with your son's teachers and review his test scores and patterns of achievement.

If you do agree that advancing his studies is an appropriate answer, make sure you include your son in on the discussion. Depending on how long he has been underachieving, then working at the appropriate aptitude level more than likely is going to be a jolt, both academically and emotionally.

First and foremost, your son's emotional and physical health are important. Right now it sounds like he's pretty happy and successful, according to basic school standards, and so are you. Working together with your son and his teachers, I suspect you'll come up with the proper answer.

Q. How can parents unknowingly contribute to their child's perfectionism?

A. Many adults who are perfectionists unknowingly contribute to the vicious cycle of perfectionism in their own children. Being aware of your own perfectionistic tendencies is a start. Then make sure your own behaviors are not instilled into your children. Become aware of parenting strategies that reward positive aspects of learning and behaviors rather than expecting perfection in your own child. Schedule time to have fun together as a family and relax. Stress-relieving exercises are a must!

Don't make your goals your child's goals. Talk, listen, and discuss your child's accomplishments, dreams, and aspirations. Work on development and success plans together.

Talk with other parents as a way of monitoring your own perfectionist behaviors. In fact, discuss this with your own children. Most children will lovingly and sincerely want to help their own parents. We are all in this process of life together.

Q. Can I as a teacher help gifted students who are perfectionists become more relaxed, or do parents play a much larger role?

A. We all play an important part in a perfectionist's life, wherever he or she may be! All children benefit from stress-relieving activities. These are some suggestions I followed as a teacher before, during, and after teaching self-contained classes for the gifted. I'm quite sure you'll find them helpful for all kids.

Each day, call a ten-minute quiet time in your room for peace and relaxation. This provides a wonderful reflection and incubation time for the creative needs of the brain. The first few days or weeks, your students will probably be fidgety, as they may not be used to this treat for deciding what they should be doing or thinking for themselves. Once this quiet time no longer is a mystery, students eagerly look forward to it. Some read, some nap, some draw, many will sit and reflect. This is a powerful and positive technique for calming and destressing perfectionists, recovering perfectionists, and all children in our classrooms.

Every Friday we would have a jogging session at the district high school track. It was walking distance from our elementary school. We'd start with ten minutes of warm-up stretches and mini-aerobic sessions right in our classroom. Then we'd walk or jog to the track, jibber-jabbering all the way.

The first two weeks, I'd start us all out with walking and then jogging, for equal distances, around the track three times. This was for teaching breathing and running techniques. There were always several students who wanted to "conquer" running the track at top speed, nonstop, two or three times the first time out. While one or two students could, the remainder of children who tried would often get cramps or become excessively winded. Besides stress relief and physical fitness, I also knew that those Friday sessions included some good life lessons for these children, like "Don't bite off more than you can chew," and "Get a lay of the land first before taking on an entire project!"

Once winter weather set in, we would at least do stretches and aerobics in the room every Friday. When spring arrived, we were back on the track. The students and I set personal goals and improved steadily. Every year some students even became avid long-distance runners. If a track was not readily accessible in some of the schools where I taught, we'd do the perimeter of the school, adding in math vocabulary lessons before we started.

Slow, deep breathing exercises once an hour are also nice stress relievers. Breathe in through the nose, 1-2-3-4; hold, 1-2-3-4; exhale through the mouth, 1-2-3-4.

Talking helps perfectionists, children and adults as well. I used to call a five-minute "talk break" every morning and afternoon. Students could ask me any questions they wanted—within reason, of course. This led to incredible thinking and discussions. Because gifted children have the ability to think and perform well beyond the norm, it is easy for them to build mountains out of molehills! Regular talks and discussions help keep irrational and unreasonable thinking in check.

I'm sure that you as a parent or teacher have your own special ways of helping to relieve many of the stresses that accompany perfectionists. How we do stress relief is not as important as doing it for perfectionists and all our students.

Q. Is procrastination a common trait among gifted students who are perfectionists?

A. Yes!

Q. Why are so many gifted children procrastinators?

A. Many times gifted children simply can't or won't face their obligations and procrastinate instead. Rather than make a mistake and not be perfect, it simply is much easier to not do the task at all. Gifted children also make mountains out of molehills. Because of their incredible ability to think and create, gifted children can't always see or imagine an end to a task, so why begin? Any assignment will never really be complete in their minds.

It is critical for us as parents and teachers to help procrastinators with time management, organization, and rational thinking. Many children simply cannot overcome this behavior on their own. We can help them!

FIVE TIPS FOR PROCRASTINATORS

1. Plot out your daily, short-term, and long-term assignments on a monthly time management sheet. Seeing the actual schedule makes the workload far less intimidating and much easier to tackle.
2. Find a quiet room in your home that you can claim at any time for studying purposes. Try to keep it organized!
3. Set aside one hour every weekend to clean your bedroom, organize your thoughts, and look over your upcoming assignments for the next week. This helps you focus and calm down!
4. Look over the coming week's TV shows and specials in your local TV guide. Allow yourself a half hour or hour a day where you can relax and unwind and watch your favorite shows. Looking forward to this treat keeps you motivated on your study tasks.
5. Plan out a tentative time of day, afternoon, or evening when you will work on your school assignments and other commitments each day. Discuss this with your parents so they can support you and help other family members respect your quiet study time. Be flexible. A large block of time on Saturdays (two hours) can help avoid the Sunday evening panic and shortage of time.

Q. How can you approach a parent who insists on trying to make their own children perfect?

A. Not easily. Parents who want their children to be perfect all the time and be successful continually fall into one or more of the following categories: adults who have never fulfilled their own dreams, so they try to live their lives through their own children; adults who are perfectionists themselves, usually due to upbringing, fear of failure, need to control, or being overly driven; adults with an inability to admit mistakes due to feelings of inadequacy or low self-esteem. Their lives are very scheduled, task-oriented, work-focused, and rigid.

Imagine trying to be a happy-go-lucky child, or just a happy child, with perfectionists as parents. No matter what you do, it's not "perfect" enough—cleaning the kitchen, mowing the lawn, doing the laundry, cleaning your room, cooking a meal, visiting grandma, washing your car, participating in school events. It's just never good enough.

Imagine the devastating blow to a child's ego. He is always admonished and told, "This wasn't done right. This is a better way!" Contrast that to, "Oh, thanks, I appreciate your way of thinking and doing things!" One approach tears the child down. The other builds him up.

Living with parents who are perfectionists is a no-win situation for the child. Often, this can lead to drinking or drugs, an inability to handle finances, failure in academics, inadequate social behaviors, or problems with personal relationships. Left without psychological intervention, depression may eventually occur.

As educators it is our moral obligation to try to help the child by talking with the parents, so that we can get permission to get counseling for the child. Most likely, the parents will be resistant. Understanding that their child needs help would be admitting that they were less than perfect parents. They may honestly not even be aware of their child's psychological suffering, even though you could write a list a mile long of abhorrent behaviors in the child's past. Denial will be the parents' defense mechanism. We can help the child by helping the parents face their denial. If only they can get him through middle school, if only they can get him through high school, if only they can get him through college—if only, if only, if only.

To assist the child by helping the parents understand and face their denial, here are a few suggestions:

1. Emphasize the child's many positive traits.
2. Review his positive academic accomplishments and standardized tests scores. If his daily scores are not in line with expectations, his standardized scores could be a start in a discussion of why. Pose this question to the parents. Even in denial, they have to have some inkling of ideas. In their heart of hearts, no parent wants his or her child to be in pain or fail.
3. Ask what the child seems to enjoy most and least about school. During this conversation, the child's perfectionist behaviors, or the parent's, should surface. Hopefully you can bring up counseling. The parents will probably feel threatened by this. However, you and they both know if an intercession can help.
4. If you don't make progress with the parents, talk one-on-one with the child. No one is better able to understand perfectionist parents that the child himself. As a trusted teacher, you can guide a child into considering counseling. If the child broaches the subject of counseling help with his parents, they might be a bit more inclined to agree.

Q. My nine-year-old son lies awake for hours each night, unable to fall asleep. Is there anything I can do to help him gain a more peaceful night's sleep?

A. When I first started teaching my Parenting the Gifted class at a local university, it rapidly became clear that many of the parents had gifted children who could not sleep well. My answer to them was talk, talk, talk! In fact, I promised that if each parent sat on his or her child's bed and talked with the child for the next seven nights, there would be no more sleep problems.

What were they to talk about? Anything. I suggested letting the child lead the conversation. Mrs. P reported that her son talked for three hours the first night, from 10:00 p.m. to 1:00 a.m. She even dozed off in the rocking chair a few times, but her son simply awakened her. By the fifth night, Roger was dozing off to a peaceful sleep after forty-five minutes of talking, and Mrs. P traded some nights with Mr. P, so she could have a full night of sleep herself!

Twelve of the fifteen parents reported positive progress with their children's sleep patterns at our next class. ☺

Q. How can I get counseling help at school for my gifted nine-year-old? He has trouble relating to his peers and is a severe perfectionist. The counseling time allotted to our school is being used up by the slower-achieving students, special education students, and troublemakers. We can't afford to pay for outside counseling services.

A. I literally had to fight for ten years to get any counseling time whatsoever for the children in my self-contained gifted classroom, and then it was only for thirty minutes a week! Gifted students have unique counseling needs, including social and emotional adjustment, perfectionism, career planning, underachievement, multipotentiality, and family relationships. First, talk to you child's teachers in gaining support for in-school counseling. Second, check your child's group IQ test results and standardized achievement test scores, or you can request an individual WISQ-R by the school psychologist. This score usually runs higher than the group normed tests. This gives you positive data as you request a fair and appropriate education for your child, including counseling. A note from your child's pediatrician requesting testing and counseling is usually beneficial, as well.

If all else fails, go to your administration and school board representatives—but always in a positive and supportive role. I know it's very frustrating at times, but keep P and P: positive and proactive.

Q. My teenage daughter seems to be crying at the slightest little happening at home. She argues constantly with her father and me, as well as with her two younger siblings, and she is sleeping much more than usual. Her grades are starting to drop, and I'm beginning to seriously worry about her. Could she be depressed or just going through the struggles of teenage years? Susan is fifteen years old.

A. Many times there is a fine line between the symptoms of excessive stress, teenage turmoil, and depression. There is a clear difference with clinical depression. This needs to be treated by a trained professional. Susan cannot just "will" her way out of clinical depression. The fact that your daughter is sleeping excessively and crying with little provocation suggests to me an immediate visit to her internist. The doctor can provide a proper diagnosis and the necessary medication, if Susan is clinically depressed.

If not, Susan still needs help dealing with the events going on in her life. So many of today's gifted children are multipotential and have excessively overloaded schedules and commitments, pursuing excellence in many of their gifted areas.

Multipotential high school children are often involved in advanced-placement classes, musical groups, debate clubs, church groups, athletics, community services, and mentorships. Coupled with an office visit to Susan's internist, please take the time to sit down with her and talk. She may be initially resistant but, after a burst of tears, she may well start blurting out the major cause of her changes in behavior, including being overwhelmed with too many activities. She may also need help with time management and study habits. The main thrust here is to get started with an intervention.

Q. What happens to gifted children? Do most succeed as adults?

A. Certainly giftedness is not a sole measure of success in life. There are a variety of variables that affect a gifted child's success as an adult. Overall, I agree with Ellen Winner's summation of the factors that predict the four possible combinations of "gifted child and adult outcomes" (1996):

1. Those gifted children most likely to develop their talent to the level of an expert will be those who have high drive and the ability to focus and derive flow from their work, those who grow up in families that combine stimulation with support, and those who are fortunate to have inspiring teachers, mentors, and role models.

2. Those gifted children most likely to leave their creative mark on a domain in adulthood will also have high drive, focus, and flow, and inspiring mentors and models. But in two other areas they should be different. They should be willing to be nonconforming, take risks, and shake up the established tradition. And they should be more likely than those who become experts to have grown up in stressful family conditions.

3. Those gifted children predicted to burn out are those whose parents push them to extremes and are overinvolved in their development.

These parents differ from those who produce creative children. Parents of future creators cause stress in their children's lives, but they are not overinvolved. Instead, they encourage independence in their offspring.

4. Those gifted children not "born into" a domain often discover their ultimate calling in adulthood, when they are catalyzed by a crystallizing experience, a life-changing event in which a gift is discovered and self-doubts are dispelled.

I personally have always fallen into the category of "should be willing to be nonconforming, take risks, and shake up the established tradition." This was not a conscious decision or easy path to follow. I was always personally and professionally true to myself and my ideals. It seemed to me to be the only way to go!

I have become increasingly aware of the need to support, guide, and direct our nonconforming, risk-taking, gifted children, teaching them strategies and the politics of how to challenge the establishment successfully. Why get your head chopped off if you can walk away with change and only a few bruises here and there?

Q. Can you recommend any books for my thirteen-year-old child to read? He is a severe perfectionist and, no matter how hard I try to help him balance his activities, the perfectionism always wins.

A. There are three books that I particularly like and have used with my graduate students as well as elementary and middle school children: *Perfectionism: What's Bad About Being Too Good?* by M. R. Adderholdt and J. Goldberg, *Fighting Invisible Tigers* by Earl Hipp, and this book. All three of these books deal with the possible underlying causes of perfectionism, suggest ways to recover, and offer a sense of humor while doing so.

Q. How can you tell when you're a recovering perfectionist?

A. These are the ways I knew for myself: You write a book about perfectionism, and on the very first page you admit to the world that you are a recovering perfectionist. You make a spelling error in a handwritten thank you note or letter. You cross out the error, correct, continue on, and mail the note. You only break out in a slight sweat rather than rewriting the entire letter!

You can laugh much more easily now than you could ever laugh before. You better understand the healthy necessity of play and having fun. It took my patient and wonderful husband fifteen years to help me understand and enjoy the fact that excellence in my work could still be a priority, while golfing, vacationing, entertaining, socializing, and enjoying our children were equally important and even more fun.

I now enjoy myself when we entertain large groups of people in our home. Before, I would be a control idiot and try to do everything for everybody throughout the party. I'd find myself regretting not having been able to talk with all of our friends and guests throughout the evening. Now I understand that adults are at a party to enjoy themselves and are perfectly capable of taking care of themselves. Don't get me wrong: my husband and I still overdo preparations, but we do have fun when the time comes.

8

ADVOCACY

One of my very favorite stories, which I use in advocacy training for the gifted, is "The Palcuzzi Ploy" (Gallagher and Gallagher 1994, 91–92). Mr. Palcuzzi, principal of Jefferson Elementary School, got tired of hearing objections to special provisions for gifted children, so he decided to spice up an otherwise mild PTA meeting with *his* proposal for gifted children. The elements of the Palcuzzi program were as follows:

1. Children should be grouped by ability.
2. Part of the school day should be given over to special instruction.
3. Talented students should be allowed time to share their talents with children of other schools in the area or even other schools throughout the state. (We will pay the transportation costs.)
4. Children should be advanced according to their talents, rather than their age.
5. These children should have specially trained and highly salaried teachers.

As might be expected, the Palcuzzi program was subjected to a barrage of criticism: "What about the youngsters who aren't able to fit into the special group; won't their egos be damaged?" "How about the cost? How can you justify transportation costs that would have to be paid by moving a special group of students from one school to another?" "Won't we be endangering the children by having them interact with others who are much more mature?"

After listening for ten or fifteen minutes, Palcuzzi said that he was not describing a *new* program for the intellectually gifted, but a program the school system had been enthusiastically supporting for a number of years—the program for *gifted basketball players*!

The irony of this story is that if a school community likes, values, and enjoys a program, protests are nonexistent. If the community does not value or support a gifted program, all sorts of protests are voiced. In most cases, you will need to positively advocate for the appropriate education of your gifted child. I can tell you right now, advocacy will be a consistent uphill journey. It helps to know your rights.

Your rights as a parent of a gifted child are the same as all other parents: You have the right to be your child's number-one advocate. You have the right to a fair and equitable education for your child. You have the right to know when local standardized tests are being given and see sample tests with questions and answers. You have the right to join your local and state PTA and advocate for the understanding, training, and support of gifted children with programming for the gifted.

As a member of your school and district PTA, you have the right to expect those organizations to schedule speakers who are experts in the field of gifted education. You have the right to know all your child's test scores and what they mean. You have the right to study sessions where differentiated curriculums and classrooms with compacted curriculums are explained to you. You have the right to expect your child's teacher to love, respect, and educate your child with the same amount of time and dedication she or he gives to all the other children in the classroom. You have the right to feel comfortable and supported by the educational system as a parent and advocate for your child, gifted children, and all children.

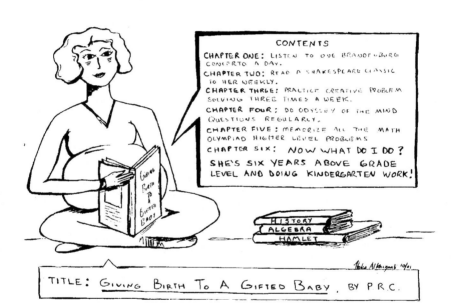

In order to best advocate for your child, know that as you work in school groups, community organizations, or neighborhood activities, there will most likely be a prejudice against the gifted. I found this throughout my career even from many of my fellow educators and administrators. Terms such as *elitist* or *egotistical* are often used in arguments against providing appropriate programs and activities for children identified as gifted. Unfortunately, this is often due to a lack of understanding of what we mean by the term. Many teachers are still not being educated in differentiating and compacting curriculums, which work for all kids, not just the gifted. Consequently, it is important for you to do your homework and familiarize yourself with the definitions and appropriate programming models and curriculum options.

Stay positive as you help other parents and teachers understand this often misunderstood field. Write your local, state, and national political leaders, requesting their help in allocating funds and resources for the gifted. Join local and state advocacy groups. On the national level, the National Association for Gifted Children (NAGC) provides conferences, publications, and current research about gifted education.

Another important point to consider is the extent to which your school district services its precocious and gifted children. You need to start asking questions and doing some research into the district's policy toward gifted children. During the past decade, significant numbers of gifted programs have been dropped in districts, some due to budget cuts and others due to the controversy and misunderstandings surrounding gifted programs. The special education inclusion model has been sweeping the country, giving equal access in heterogeneously grouped classrooms to identified special education students and remedial students. A special education teacher "pushes in" to help the regular classroom teacher with the extra classroom numbers, workload, and classroom management. But who is there to help differentiate and cognitively challenge the gifted?

There are some basic steps and information gathering I encourage you to do before meeting with your children's teachers in your school district:

- Talk with other parents in your neighborhood, church, and athletic club, anywhere you can find them, asking what they particularly like about their children's schooling, including teachers, class sizes, intellectual clubs, community service organizations, fitness programs, and social activities. Of particular interest to you would be the district's attitude/programming service for gifted children.

- Find out if the rights of gifted children and gifted education are protected by law in your state. Currently about 50 percent of the states legally protect the right to an appropriate education for their gifted children.
- Question your children regularly on what they especially enjoy and don't enjoy about school. Are they learning new things or studying lessons and materials they already know? Is a part of every day being used by them to help slower-learning or remedial students? If they finish assignments early, are they required to then go to one of the learning centers in their room, or are they given choices?
- Is the curriculum differentiated for them, or are they given more and harder work?
- Have an idea in mind as to what changes and challenges would benefit your children before meeting with their teachers. Change almost always comes slowly, especially in school districts, which are commonly entrenched in a history of rules, bureaucracy, and regulations.
- Always meet with your children's teachers *first*! Nothing antagonizes a teacher more than being called in by the principal concerning a parent meeting that occurred without him or her. No one enjoys being blindsided—not the teacher, not you, not the administrator, not your children!

A wonderful new book has just been published through the NAGC: *Aiming for Excellence: Gifted Program Standards*, by M. Landrum, C. Callahan, and B. Shaklee. It benchmarks standards of excellence in seven critical areas: program design, program administration and management, socioemotional guidance and counseling, student identification, curriculum and instruction, professional development, and program evaluation. The authors understand the current standards, providing examples, benefits, outcomes, and possible barriers to the successful implementation of the standards. Find this book, read it carefully, and you'll be much better equipped intellectually and emotionally as you approach your children's teachers and administrators.

I must admit, I secretly always hoped that a brave and courageous family would turn to the legal system to help its cognitively gifted children get a fair and appropriate education, once our school district had dropped its gifted-and-talented program. It would also have helped me help them. There are three sources that I would like you to familiarize yourself with before you undertake the legal system for support.

First, the *Jacob K. Javits Gifted and Talented Students Education Act of 1988, Part B.* Keep a copy of this with you, and/or memorize the Statement of Purpose on page 169. You'll learn there has been and continues to be hundreds of thousands of dollars allocated to major colleges, universities, and school districts throughout our country since the inception of the Jacob K. Javits Gifted and Talented Students Education Act of 1988 for the research, demonstration, teacher training, and similar activities related to gifted education. Investigate your local districts to see what funds and programs or projects are available for your children, parents, and local educators.

This act provides financial assistance to state and local agencies, institutions of higher education, and other public and private agencies and organizations, and it initiates a coordinated program of research, demonstration projects, personnel training, and similar activities designed to build a nationwide capability in elementary and secondary schools to identify and meet the special educational needs of gifted and talented students. It is also the purpose of this act to supplement and make more effective the expenditure of state and local funds and of federal funds made available under Chapter 2 of Title I and Title II of this act, for the education of gifted and talented students.

Simply stated, there have been and continue to be hundreds of thousands of dollars allocated to colleges, universities, and school districts throughout our country, since the inception of the Jacob K. Javits Gifted and Talented Students Education Act of 1988, for the research, demonstration, teacher training, and similar activities related to gifted education. Investigate your local district to see what funds and programs or projects are available for your children and local educators.

Second is *Gifted Children and the Law: Mediation, Due Process, and Court Cases,* by F. Karnes and R. Marquardt. This text is a valuable resource and major contribution in the advocacy for gifted education. It provides the results of legal action and reinforces a free and appropriate education for exceptional children (P.L. 94-142, the Education for All Handicapped Children Act). Parents can read about cases in which the courts clearly ruled in favor of parents and their gifted children.

WHO MURDERED THE MINDS OF GIFTED CHILDREN?

PROFESSOR DULL, IN THE CLASSROOM, WITH REPETITIVE DRILLS

Third, *Gifted Children and Legal Issues in Education: Parents' Stories of Hope*, also by F. Karnes and R. Marquardt, is a wonderful resource for parents and teachers, who have become exhausted and exasperated as well in trying to accomplish an appropriate education for their gifted and talented children and students. Filled with a compilation of personal stories by parents of gifted children, this book lends support to parents by recounting successfully settled disputes by parents with the determination and fortitude to achieve excellence in education for their own children and all children.

An additional way you could help advocate for a better understanding of gifted children and their appropriate education within your school, community, and state is to help develop a Gifted Child Awareness Week. Working in conjunction with your district's staff development coordinator and local, county, or state administrators would allow you better access to funds in support of speakers, advertising, and refreshments. Here is a possible model for you to follow:

Gifted Child Awareness Week

All parents and educators are invited to attend.

Monday
    Continental Breakfast provided by the PTA
    Speaker: Dr. Rosemary Callard-Szulgit, 8:00 a.m
    Topic: Parenting and Teaching the Gifted

Tuesday
    Luncheon provided by [your state] Chapter in Support of Gifted Education
    Speaker: Dr. Carol Tomlinson
    Topic: Curriculum Differentiation

Wednesday
    Dinner provided by BOCES in Support of Educating the Gifted, 5:30 p.m.
    Speaker: Dr. Ellen Winner
    Topic: Myths and Realities of Gifted Children

Thursday
    Brunch provided by your school's administration
    Speaker: Dr. Jim Delisle
    Topic: Creativity and Gifted Children

Friday
    Rally, 7:00 p.m.
    Speaker: Dr. Rosemary Callard-Szulgit
    Topic: What Works for Gifted Works for All!

Sarah Heindel
Gifted / Talented

PROMOTING CREATIVITY IN YOUR GIFTED CHILDREN

- Encourage and support uniqueness.
- Provide quiet time and space daily for your child to rest and reflect. This allows incubation time for his or her brain, which then enhances creative thinking.
- Encourage humor, telling jokes, making up jokes, putting a positive twist on things. ☹→☺
- When your child is served lemons, see how many different ways you can make lemonade together.
- Take day trips to local historical museums, art museums, music schools, and local industries, reflecting together on patterns, uniqueness, and observations.
- Talk, discuss, talk, discuss, talk, discuss, and reflect together often.
- Bedtime is a good time to sit and discuss whatever is currently on your child's mind.
- Encourage overnights with your child's creative friends, at your house and theirs.
- Provide lessons for your child in the area of his or her expertise, talent, and desires.
- Read and discuss the Newbery Medal–winning books together. They're filled with life lessons, gifted thinkers, mystery, and intrigue. I especially recommend *Maniac Magee, Dear Mr. Henshaw, From the Mixed-Up Files of Mrs. Basil E. Frankweiler, Mrs. Frisby and the Rats of NIMH, The Egypt Game, Holes, Shiloh,* and *Bridge to Terabithia.*
- If your child is artistically inclined, read the Caldecott Medal–winning books. They have absolutely beautiful illustrations. Encourage your child to design alternative cover illustrations for the Caldecotts and enter them in local art contests. The Caldecotts are also wonderful for spurring creative writing in your child, no matter what age.
- Discuss the concepts and processes of intuition, creativity, hunches, imagery, brainstorming, creative problem solving, Bloom's taxonomy, love, spirituality, morals, values, and passion at dinnertime together. This family time together was always my favorite with my husband and four children. I looked forward to it every day and learned so much!

9

GIFTED CHILDREN SPEAK TO US

Gifted children talk about being gifted, other children, parents, teachers, school, thinking, America.

For years, every summer I coordinated a two-week cultural arts course for gifted nine-to-thirteen-year-olds in our county. The children and I always had a wonderful time together. On the very last morning, I would take a peaceful hour with them—soft lights, easy music—and tell the story of Kahlil Gibrans's *The Prophet*. I would then ask the children to honor me by being my prophets, answering some of the age-old questions of humankind.

I don't believe I ever underestimated the abilities of my students, but I never ceased to be awed by them. Following are just a few of the hundreds of responses I received. I'm sure you'll enjoy them as much as the parents and I did.

A GIFTED CHILD

SPEAK TO ME ABOUT BEING GIFTED

To me, it means something special, something unique. You don't need to get great grades or be very smart. You are gifted if you want to touch the sky, if you want to stretch the limit. If you follow your spirit, your heart, your mind, you are gifted. (Jessica, age 11)

Many people wonder what gifted means. It is my belief that it truly has no specific meaning. It may mean you are talented or smart, or maybe just proud of who you are. You can stretch the limits of this word and make it fit your spirit. (Kat, age 10)

Gifted means being blessed by God with something special. (Steven, age 12)

I think being gifted means having an IQ of 135 or more. (Frank, age 9)

A gifted student is a person who is above the clouds and cannot see the ground from where he started from but can see his destination in the stars. (Carl, age 11)

SPEAK TO ME ABOUT CHILDREN

Children are like the seeds of the future to me. They are the people who will change the world tomorrow, and they will succeed in doing so. They are different from adults in a way that they stretch their hands out to the stars and try new things. They are free at heart, mind, and spirit. (Jessica, age 11)

Children are young adults who have a lot to learn before they grow up. (Eric, age 10)

Children are little people that haven't learned everything about life. They also make more mistakes than adults. (Alex, age 10)

Children are all the members of a particular species that have a mother and father. (Steven, age 12)

Children are people who have very little responsibilities. They can run and play and learn every minute, every instant. They are the plaster, still sifting into the mold, not yet complete. (Molly, age 10)

A child is anybody who is 18 years old or younger. (Frank, age 9)

Children are very mentally and physically fragile. (Andrew, age 11)

SPEAK TO ME ABOUT PARENTS

Parents are like the sun which nourishes the seed. They love and care for their children, watch them grow, and watch them change the world. Parents bring life into the world and raise it. They are the leaders of their children, who will be the leaders of theirs. They guide us through the hard times, the times when we don't have faith. (Jessica, age 11)

Parents guide us to our health, our faith, our life. They shape us to be who we are, teach us right from wrong. They are our mothers who brought us onto this earth and the fathers who teach us sports and how to be tough and not to give up. They are our leaders. (Kat, age 10)

Parents are people who try to do the best for their children. (Eric, age 10)

Parents are important people because they help children grow and learn so that they can take their rightful places in the world. Without parents, children wouldn't get the nurturing they need. (Jeffrey, age 11)

Parents are people who can help you when things seem hopeless. Children also reflect their parents. (Andrew, age 11)

Parents are people who shine light on the path of life, even though they cannot walk the whole journey with their children. (Carl, age 11)

Parents are people who gave you birth and boss you around. (Katie, age 9)

SPEAK TO ME ABOUT TEACHERS

Teachers are more than just people who tutor you in math, writing, and history. They teach you the precious things which will bond with you for as long as you live. Anyone is a teacher; parents, schoolteachers, friends, even children. They all help us grow joyously and well. Teachers are filled with love and care. They are friends to their students and all who know them. (Jessica, age 11)

Teachers are people who teach you and help you progress in life; if they are good ones, they will care how you're doing in school. (Andrew, age 11)

SPEAK TO ME ABOUT SCHOOL

School is a building filled with learning. It overflows with children who reach to the sky and succeed. It's where friendship sprouts and people come together into one. When I think of a school, a ring of children holding hands and learning comes to mind. School is a building of courage, trying new things, friendship, and learning. (Jessica, age 11)

School is where people of all ages go to learn new things and be taught the skills that they need in the world. (Jeffrey, age 11)

School can change the lives of millions because it is the place where teachers teach, the children learn, and the cultural world grows. (Molly, age 10)

School is a place where children go to learn things to help them in life. Sometimes people who aren't very good in school don't like school and good students like it better. (Elise, age 11)

School is a place where learning is the key and being with friends is an especially fun part. (Aileen, age 9)

School is a place where average students learn. Gifted students learn anywhere else. (Carl, age 11)

SPEAK TO ME ABOUT THINKING

Thinking is like a seedling which grows through the tangle of my mind. It keeps on flourishing, until it bursts from its shell onto a sheet of paper. Like a waterfall, it keeps on pouring. When a dream forms, I flow with it, wherever it may go. I can travel to the moon if I think about it. Thought is the beginning of a wonderful journey which can take you anywhere in the world. (Jessica, age 11)

Thinking: What is 2 + 2? If you answered, you were just thinking. (Kat, age 10)

Thinking is when you use your wits to figure out the answer to a problem. (Alex, age 10)

Thinking is when anyone in the world has a thought and studies it in their brain. It is how we come up with ideas that make the world better. (Jeffrey, age 11)

Thinking is what you do when you are trying to figure something out or trying to get an idea. (Julie, age 10)

Thinking is what you do all the time. You have to think about everything you do. You have to think about what question you want to ask me. (Ben, age 11)

AMERICA

By Carl Adair, Age 10

My country tis' of thee
Ringing bells of
freedom unite your
states of
being.
The vastness of your
beauty radiates
Strength and courage
within our
hearts.
Your many cultures
Races,
Religions,
Are a
Rainbow
Projected through
The prism of
Immigration,
Whose artists,
Musicians, and
Scientists,
Make up your nature.
Yet your honorable
Record is not without
Blemishes
Fractures litter your
Surface of bronze,
Paining with the
Violence
Our hates have created.
Americans of different
Color, race or thinking listen

To each other with
Misunderstanding.
Yet the magnificence of your
Freedom dwarfs this and
The other problems
That have survived and grown
Through the decades of striving
For excellence.
Too often your inhabitants
Take for granted the
Fact they have their own
One among many others.
These tones, when played
Together, not only ring true in perfect
Harmony,
But the awesome chorus of our
American Society.
Sweet land of liberty
Of thee I sing.

> "Art opens up
>
> the magic of the mind."
>
> **—Wendy Gribb**

APPENDIX

Resources

PROFESSIONAL ASSOCIATIONS AND ADVOCACY GROUPS FOR GIFTED EDUCATION

American Association for Gifted Children
(Talented Identification Program)
Duke University
1121 West Main St., Ste. 100
Durham, NC 27701
(919) 683-1400

American Mensa, Ltd.
2626 East 14th St.
Brooklyn, NY 11235

Association for the Gifted
Council for Exceptional Children
1920 Association Dr.
Reston, VA 22091
(800) 336-3278

The Institute for Law and Gifted Education
909 South 34th Ave.
Hattiesburg, MS 39402

National Association for Creative Children and Adults
8080 Springvalley Dr.
Cincinnati, OH 43236
(513) 631-1777

National Association for Gifted Children
1155 15th St., N.W., Ste. 1002
Washington, DC 20005
(202) 785-4268

National Association of State Boards of Education
526 Hall of the States
444 North Capital St., N.W.
Washington, DC 20001
(202) 624-5845

Supporting the Emotional Needs of Gifted (SENG)
P.O. Box 6550
Scottsdale, AZ 85261
(602) 498-6744

World Council for Gifted and Talented Children, Inc.
18401 Hiawatha Street
Northridge, CA 91326
(818) 368-7501

ADDITIONAL RESOURCES

Association for the Education of Gifted Underachieving Students (AEGUS)
4414 S. Eagle Village Rd.
Manlius, NY 13104
(205) 348-7340

Council for Exceptional Children
1920 Association Dr.
Reston, VA 22901
(703) 620-3660
www.cec.sped.org

National Research Center on the Gifted and Talented
University of Connecticut
2131 Hillside Rd., U-7
Storrs, CT 06269
(860) 486-4676
www.gifted.uconn.edu/nrcgt.html

Parent Information Network for the Gifted (PING)
190 Rock Rd.
Glen Park, NJ 07542
(900) 773-7464

INTERNET RESOURCES

Birth Order Home Page
www.ncn.net/~cliffi/index.htm
Connects to topics of birth order comparisons, characteristics, and tests.

Education Program for Gifted Youth (EPGY)
http://kanpai.stanford.edu/epgy

Eric Clearinghouse for Exceptional Children
www.aspensys.com/eric/index.html

Exceptional Parent Magazine Online
http://www.apsmagazine.com/parentmagazine/
Information, support, and ideas to families of children with disabilities.

Family Education Network
http://familyeducation.com/email

The Gifted Child Society
www.gifted.org

Talented and Gifted (TAG) Resources Home Page
www.eskimo.com/~user/kids.html

Hoagies' Gifted Education
www.hoagiesgifted.org

Institute for the Academic Advancement of Youth, Center for Talented Youth
www.jhu.edu:80/~gifted

National Resource Center on the Gifted and Talented (NRC/GT)
www.ucc.ucon.edu:80/~wwwgt

The Page of Procrastination
www.angelfire.com/mi/society

Parenthoodweb.com
An award-winning online parenting, pregnancy, and family community for parents and prospective parents. Free expert advice, discussion and chat groups, polls, recall information, and birth announcements.

Procrastination Research Group
www.carleton.cal%7Etpyehyl/index.html

The Tag Family Network
www.telport.com/~rKaltwas/tag

Yahoo Resources for Gifted Youth K–12
www.yahoo.com/text/education/K_12/Gifted_Youth

JOURNALS AND MAGAZINES

Advanced Development
Gifted Development Center
1452 Marion Street
Denver, CO 80218
(303) 837-8778

Creative Children and Adult Quarterly
8080 Spring Valley Dr.
Cincinnati, OH 45236
(513) 631-1777

Gifted Child Quarterly
1155 15th St. N.W., Ste. 1002
Washington, DC 20005
(202) 785-4268

Gifted Child Today
P.O. Box 8813
Waco, TX 76714
(800) 998-2208

Journal of Creative Behavior
Creative Education Foundation
1050 Union Rd., #4
Buffalo, NY 14224
(800) 447-2774

Journal for the Education of the Gifted
University of North Carolina Press
P.O. Box 2288
Chapel Hill, NC 27515

Journal for the Education of the Gifted
Council for Exceptional Children
1920 Association Dr.
Reston, VA 22091

Mensa Research Journal
1229 Corporate Drive West
Arlington, TX 76006-6103
(817) 607-0060, ext. 123

Parenting for High Potential
1707 L St. N.W., Ste. 550
Washington, DC 20036
(202) 785-4268

Roeper Review
Roeper City and County Schools
P.O. Box 329
Bloomfield Hills, MI 48303
(313) 642-1500

STATE ORGANIZATIONS

Alabama Association for Gifted Children, www.aagc.freeservers.com/
aagc.html
Arizona Association for the Gifted, www.aagt.org
Arizona Association for Gifted and Talented, www.azagt.org
Arkansans for Gifted and Talented Education, pollyb@af.affc.k12.ar.us
California Association for the Gifted (CAG), www.CAGifted.org
Colorado Association for the Gifted, CAGT@aol.com
Connecticut Association for the Gifted and Talented, www.CTGifted.org
Delaware Talented and Gifted Association, mdee@state.de.us
Florida Association for the Gifted (FLAG) and Parents for Able Learner Students, members.aol.com/pals222
Georgia Association for Gifted Children, www.gagc.org
Hawaii Gifted Association, P.O. Box 22878, Honolulu, HI 96823, (808)
732-1138
Idaho—The Association for the Gifted (ITAG), coehp.idbsu.edu/itagsage
Illinois Association for Gifted Children (IAGC), www.IAGCGifted.org
Indiana Association for the Gifted, www.iag-online.org

Iowa Talented and Gifted Association, www.uiowa.edu/~itag

Kansas Association for the Gifted, Talented and Creative, www.KGTC.org

Kentucky Association for Gifted Education (KAGE), www.wku.edu/KAGE

Louisiana Association for Gifted and Talented Students (AGTS), www.hal. calc.k12.la.us/~gifted/gifted.html

Maine Educators Gifted and Talented (MEGAT), www.sad28.k12.me.us

Maryland Coalition for Gifted and Talented Education, jroache@ids2. idsonline.com

Massachusetts Association for Gifted Education (MAGE), www. MASSGifted.org

Michigan Alliance for Gifted Education (MAGE), www.MIGiftedchild.org

Minnesota Council for the Gifted and Talented, www.MCGT.net

Minnesota Educators of the Gifted and Talented, www.informns.k12. us/~megt

Mississippi Association for Gifted Children (MAGC), www.magc.org

Gifted Association of Missouri (GAM), www.mogam.org

Montana Association of Gifted and Talented Education, www.members. home.net/cabreras/agate.htm

Nebraska Association for the Gifted, www.NebraskaGifted.org

Nevada Association for Gifted and Talented (NAGT), 14101 Old Virginia Rd., Reno, NV 89511, (775) 852-8209, asprinkle@washoe.k12.nv.us

New Hampshire Association for Gifted Children, P.O. Box 786, Hollis, NH 03049, (603) 882-3512, Gifteacher@aol.com

New Jersey Association for Gifted Children, www.NJAGC.org

Advocacy for Gifted and Talented Education in New York (AGATE), www.agateny.org

North Carolina Association for the Gifted and Talented (NCAGT), www. ncagt.org

Ohio Association for Gifted Children (OAGC), www.oagc.com

Oklahoma Association for Gifted, Creative and Talented, 810 SW 23rd St., El Reno, OK 73036, (405) 262-2765

Oregon Association for Talented & Gifted (OATAG), www.oatag.org

Pennsylvania Association for Gifted Education (PAGE), www.penngifted. org

Rhode Island Gifted and Talented, www.ri.net/gifted_talented/rhode.html

South Carolina Consortium Gifted Education, www.SCCGE.org

South Dakota Association for Gifted Education, 2006 Buena Vista Dr., Rapid City, SD 57702, (605) 394-4031, silvermn@rapidnet.com

Tennessee Association for the Gifted (TAG), www.tag-tenn.org

Texas Association for the Gifted and Talented (TAGT), www.txgifted.org

Utah Association for Gifted Children (UAGC), www.uagc.org

Vermont Network for the Gifted, University of Vermont, C-150 Living Learning Center, Burlington, VT 05405, (802) 985-3405

Virginia Association of the Gifted (VAG), www.vagifted.org

Washington Association of Educators of the Talented and Gifted (WAETG), www.WAETG.org

Washington Coalition for Gifted Education, Northwest Gifted Child Association, www.innw.net/explorers/nwgac.htm

West Virginia Association for Gifted and Talented, www.geocities.com/athens/olympus/4764/wvagt.html

Wisconsin Association for Talented and Gifted (WATG), www.focol.org/~watg

MAGAZINES THAT PUBLISH CHILDREN'S WORKS

Creative Kids is the nation's largest magazine by and for kids. The magazine bursts with games, stories, and opinions all by and for kids ages eight to fourteen. You will find fun activities like brain teasers, contests, stories, poetry, pen pals, mysteries, and more. This interactive magazine also includes activities that stimulate and encourage the creativity of readers. Kids from all over the world read and contribute to *Creative Kids*. The magazine includes examples of the most creative student work to be found in any publication. Kids express themselves in letters to the editor, answers to posed questions, and questions of their own. www.prufrock.com.

Stone Soup, the Magazine by Young Writers and Artists (ages eight to thirteen), is the only magazine made up entirely of the creative work of children. Young people from all over the world contribute stories, poems, book reviews, and artwork to the magazine. Published six times a year. Contains no advertising. www.stonesoup.com

Skipping Stones is a nonprofit children's magazine that contains stories, articles, and photos from all over the world. The magazine accepts art and original writing in all languages and from all ages. Non-English writings are accompanied by English translations to encourage the learning of other languages. Each issue also contains international pen pals, book reviews, news, and a guide for parents and teachers. Published bimonthly during the school year. www.skippingstones.org

Cicada, the Literary Magazine for Teenagers and Young Adults (ages fourteen and up), publishes original short stories, poems, and first-person essays and encourages submissions from readers. Published six times per year. www.cicadamag.com

Kidnews.com is a free news and writing service for students and teachers from around the globe. It has published thousands of young authors from every continent (except Antartica). Anyone may submit a review, journalism piece, short story, poem, sports critique, real-life account, opinion, or advice to fellow kids. Every submission is edited and reviewed for content and language before being posted. Kids can also find a pen pal on this site. www.kidnews.com

REFERENCES

Adderholdt-Elliott, M. 1990. "A Comparison of the 'Stress Seeker' and the 'Perfectionist.'" *Gifted Child Today* (May/June): 50–51.

Adderholdt, M. R., and J. Goldberg. 1999. *Perfectionism: What's Bad About Being Too Good?* Minneapolis: Free Spirit.

Bernardo, D. 1990. "Competitive Overdrive Stalls High-Achieving Teens." *Gifted Child Today* (May/June): 30–31.

Betts, G. T. 1986. "Development of the Emotional and Social Needs of Gifted Individuals." *Journal of Counseling and Development* 64: 587–89.

Delisle, J., and J. Galbraith. 2002. *When Gifted Kids Don't Have All the Answers: How to Meet Their Social and Emotional Needs.* Minneapolis: Free Spirit.

Emmett, J., and C. Minor. 1993. "Career Decision-Making Factors in Gifted Young Adults." *Career Development Quarterly* 41: 350–65.

Gallagher, J., and Gallagher, S. 1994. "The Palcuzzi Ploy." *Teaching the Gifted*: 91–92.

Gardner, H. 1993. *Multiple Intelligences: The Theory in Practice.* New York: Basic Books.

Goldberg-Edelson, M. 1995. "Autism-Related Disorders in DSM-IV." Retrieved March 22, 2001, from Center for the Study of Autism website: http://www.autism.org/dms.html.

Hess, L. 1994. "Life, Liberty and the Pursuit of Perfection." *Gifted Child Today* (May/June): 28–31.

Landrum, M., C. Callahan, and B. Shaklee. 2001. *Aiming for Excellence: Gifted Program Standards*. Waco, Tex.: Prufrock Press.

Little, C. 2002. "Which Is It? Asperger's Syndrome or Giftedness: Defining the Differences." *Gifted Child Today* (winter): 58–63.

Ross, P., ed. 1993. *National Excellence: A Case for Developing America's Talent*. Washington, D.C.: U.S. Department of Education.

Weisse, D. 1990. "Gifted Adolescents and Suicide." *The School Counselor* 37: 351–57.

Winner, E. 1996. *Gifted Children: Myths and Realities*. New York: Basic Books.

BIBLIOGRAPHY

Ablard, K. E., and W. D. Parker. "Parents' Achievement Goals and Perfectionism in Their Academically Talented Children." *Journal of Youth and Adolescence* 26 (1997): 65–66.

Adderholdt-Elliott, M. "Perfectionism and Underachievement." *Gifted Child Today* (January/February 1989): 19–21.

——. "A Comparison of the 'Stress Seeker' and the 'Perfectionist.'" *Gifted Child Today* (May/June 1990): 50–51.

Adderholdt, M. R., and J. Goldberg. *Perfectionism: What's Bad About Being Too Good?* Minneapolis: Free Spirit, 1999.

Austin, A. B., and D. C. Draper. "Peer Relationships of the Academically Gifted: A Review." *Gifted Child Quarterly* 25, no. 3 (1981): 129–34.

Baker, J. A. "Everyday Stressors of Academically Gifted Adolescents." *Journal of Secondary Gifted Education* 7 (1996): 356–68.

Benbow, C. P. "Meeting the Needs of Gifted Students through Acceleration: A Neglected Resource." Pp. 23–36 in *Emerging Programs*. Vol. 4 of *Handbook of Special Education: Research and Practice*, ed. M. C. Wang, M. C. Reynolds, and H. J. Walberg. Elmsford, N.Y.: Pergamon Press, 1991.

——. Acceleration as a Method for Meeting the Academic Needs of Intellectually Talented Children. Pp. 279–94 in *Excellence in Educating Gifted and Talented Learners*, ed. J. Van Tassel-Baska. Denver: Love, 1998.

Bernardo, D. "Competitive Overdrive Stalls High-Achieving Teens." *Gifted Child Today* (May/June 1990): 30–31.

Betts, G. T. "Development of the Emotional and Social Needs of Gifted Individuals." *Journal of Counseling and Development* 64 (1986): 587–89.

Bloom, Benjamin, ed. *Taxonomy of Educational Objectives: Handbook of the Cognitive Domain.* New York: Longman, 1984.

Brophy, B. "Workaholics Beware: Long Hours May Not Pay." *U.S. News and World Report,* April 7, 1986, 60.

Burns, D. D. "The Perfectionist's Script for Self-Defeat." *Psychology Today,* November 1980, 70–76.

Callahan, C., and C. A. Tomlinson. *Heterogeneity: Inclusion or Delusion? Can We Make Academically Diverse Classrooms Succeed?* Alexandria, Va.: Association for Supervision and Curriculum Development, 1996.

Callard-Szulgit, R. *Parenting and Teaching the Gifted.* Lanham, Md.: Scarecrow Press, 2003.

Carlson, Richard. *Don't Sweat the Small Stuff . . . and It's All Small Stuff.* New York: Hyperion, 1997.

Clark, W. H., and N. E. Hankins. "Giftedness and Conflict." *Roeper Review* 8 (1985): 50–53.

Cohen, L. M., and E. Frydenberg. *Coping for Capable Kids: Strategies for Parents, Teachers, and Students.* Waco, Tex.: Prufrock Press, 1996.

Colangelo, N. "Counseling Gifted Students: Issues and Practices." Pp. 353–65 in *Handbook of Gifted Education,* 2d ed., ed. N. Colangelo and G. A. Davis. Boston: Allyn and Bacon, 1997.

Cross, Tracy L. "Putting the Well-Being of All Students (Including Gifted Students) First." *Gifted Child Today* (fall 2002): 14–17.

Cross, T. L. *On the Social and Emotional Lives of Gifted Children.* Waco, Tex.: Prufrock Press, 2001.

Cymerman, S., and D. Modest. *SAGE: The Spice of Learning for Gifted and Talented.* Longmont, Colo.: Sopris West, 1994.

Delisle, J., and J. Galbraith. *When Gifted Kids Don't Have All the Answers: How to Meet Their Social and Emotional Needs.* Minneapolis: Free Spirit, 2002.

Ehrlich, S. *Rationales for Funding Gifted Education.* Minneapolis: Minnesota Council for the Gifted and Talented, 2001.

Elkind, D. *The Hurried Child: Growing Up Too Fast Too Soon.* Reading, Mass.: Addison-Wesley, 1981.

———. *All Grown Up and No Place To Go: Teenagers in Crisis.* Reading, Mass.: Addison Wesley Longman, 1997.

Emmett, J., and C. Minor. "Career Decision-Making Factors in Gifted Young Adults." *Career Development Quarterly* 41 (1993): 350–65.

Feldheusen, J. F. "Why the Public Schools Will Continue to Neglect the Gifted." *Gifted Child Today* 12, no. 2 (1989): 56–59.

Freeman, J. "Some Emotional Aspects of Being Gifted." *Journal for the Education of the Gifted* 17, no. 2 (1994): 180–97.

Gardner, H. *Frames of Mind: The Theory of Multiple Intelligences.* New York: Basic Books, 1984.

———. *Multiple Intelligences: The Theory in Practice.* New York: Basic Books, 1993.

Garland, A. F., and E. Zigler. "Emotional and Behavioral Problems Among Highly Intellectually Gifted Youth." *Roeper Review* 22 (1999): 41–44.

Hess, L. "Life, Liberty and the Pursuit of Perfection." *Gifted Child Today* (May/June 1994): 28–31.

Hipp, E. *Fighting Invisible Tigers: A Stress Management Guide for Teens.* Minneapolis: Free Spirit, 1995.

Karnes, F., and R. Marquardt, eds. *Gifted Children and Legal Issues in Education: Parents Stories of Hope.* Dayton: Ohio Psychology Press, 1991.

Khatena, J. *Educational Psychology of the Gifted.* New York: Wiley, 1982.

Kerr, B. *A Handbook for Counseling the Gifted and Talented.* Alexandria, Va.: American Counseling Association, 1991.

———. *Smart Girls, Women and Giftedness.* Scottsdale, Az.: Great Potential Press, 1996.

———. *Smart Girls: A New Psychology of Girls, Women, and Giftedness.* Scottsdale, Ariz.: Gifted Psychology Press, 1997.

Kerr, B., and S. Cohn. *Smart Boys: Talent, Manhood, and the Search for Meaning.* Scottsdale, Ariz.: Great Potential Press, 2001.

Landrum, M., C. Callahan, and B. Shaklee. *Aiming for Excellence: Gifted Program Standards.* Waco, Tex.: Prufrock Press, 2001.

Leman, K. *The Birth Order Book: Why You Are the Way You Are.* New York: Dell, 1985.

Mackinnon, Donald W. *In Search of Human Effectiveness: Identifying and Developing Creativity.* Buffalo, N.Y.: Creative Education Foundations, 1978.

Moon, S. M., K. R. Kelly, and J. F. Feldhusen. "Specialized Counseling Services for Gifted Youth and Their Families: A Needs Assessment." *Gifted Child Quarterly* 41 (1997): 16–25.

Nugent, S. A. "Perfectionism: Its Manifestations and Classroom-Based Interventions." *Journal of Secondary Gifted Education* 11 (2002): 215–21.

Parker, W. D., and C. J. Mills. "The Incidence of Perfectionism in Gifted Children." *Gifted Quarterly* 40 (1996): 194–99.

Piechowski, M. M. "Developmental Potential." Pp. 25–27 in *New Voices in Counseling the Gifted*, ed. N. Colangelo and R. T. Zaffran. Dubuque, Iowa: Kendall/Hunt, 1997.

Pufal-Struzik, I. "Self-Actualization and Other Personality Dimensions and Predictors of Mental Health of Intellectually Gifted Students." *Roeper Review* 22 (1999): 44–47.

Reis, S. M. "How Schools Are Shortchanging the Gifted." *Technology Review* 97, no. 3 (1994): 38–45.

———. "Providing Equity for All: Meeting the Needs of High Ability Students." Pp. 119–31 in *Beyond Tracking: Finding Success in Inclusive Schools*, ed. Harbison Dod and Jane A. Page. Bloomington, Ind.: Phi Delta Kappa, 1995.

Reis, S. M, D. E. Burns, and J. S. Renzulli. *Curriculum Compacting: The Complete Guide to Modifying the Regular Curriculum for High-Ability Students*. Mansfield, Conn.: Creative Learning Press, 1992.

Reis, S. M., J. Westberg, J. Kulikowich, F. Caillard, T. Hebert, J.H. Purcell, J. Rogers, J. Swist, and J. Plucker. *An Analysis of Curriculum Compacting on Classroom Practices: Technical Report*. Storrs, Conn.: National Research Center on the Gifted and Talented, 1992.

Rimm, S. B. 1993. "Gifted Kids Have Feelings Too." *Gifted Child Today* (January-February 1993): 20–24.

Ross, P., ed. *National Excellence: A Case for Developing America's Talent*. Washington, D.C.: U.S. Department of Education, 1993.

Schwartz, L. L. "Educating the Gifted to the Gifted: A National Resource. Pp. 1–7 in *Why Give "Gifts" to the Gifted: Investing in a National Resource*. Thousand Oaks, Calif.: Corwin Press, 1994.

Shroeder-Davis, S. "Giftedness: A Double-Edged-Sword." *Book Links* (March 1994): 25.

Sternberg, R. 1997. "What Does It Mean To Be Smart?" *Educational Leadership* 54, no. 6 (1997): 20–24.

Tomlinson, Carol. *The Differentiated Classroom: Responding to the Needs of All Learners*. Alexandria, Va.: Association for Supervision and Curriculum Development, 1999.

Treffinger, D. J., C. Callahan, and V. L. Baughn. "Research on Enrichment Efforts in Gifted Education." Pp. 37–55 in *Emerging Programs*. Vol. 4 of *Handbook of Special Education: Research and Practice*, ed. M. C. Wang, M. C. Reynolds, and H. J. Walberg. Oxford: Pergamon Press, 1991.

Webb, J., E. Meckstroth, and S. Tolan. *Guiding the Gifted Child*. Columbus, Ohio: Psychology Press, 1993.

Weisse, D. "Gifted Adolescents and Suicide." *The School Counselor* 37 (1990): 351–57.

Winebrenner, S. *Teaching Gifted Kids in the Regular Classroom*. Minneapolis: Free Spirit, 1992.

Winner, E. *Gifted Children: Myths and Realities*. New York: Basic Books, 1996.

Whitmore, Alyn. *Giftedness, Conflict and Underachievement*. Needham Heights, Mass.: Allyn & Bacon, 1980.

Zukav, Gary. *The Heart of the Soul*. New York: Simon & Schuster, 2001.

INDEX